Black Bride of the Vineyards

God's Love for Black People

– ARTIEL NHEMA –

"This book expertly weaves the Old and New Testaments into a clear image of a God of purpose in black people's lives. This is the message that black Christians have been waiting for."

Bishop Lewin Takavarasha, New Anointing Ministries Zimbabwe.

FASTPRINT PUBLISHING
PETERBOROUGH, ENGLAND

BLACK BRIDE OF THE VINEYARDS

Printed in England by

www.printondemand-worldwide.com

COVER DESIGN BY
DiamondDefinition.co.uk

ACKNOWLEDGEMENTS

My wife Tsitsi for sharing my experiences and questions about black people and colonialism

My children Dean, Becky and Michael for being comfortable in their black skin and part of the new generation of hope that finds no need to see or feel colour in people.

Inspirational princes of black people who pastor great congregations all over the world, mention of whose names would belittle others just as deserving of mention as them

Inspirational non-black pastors and writers who have been worthy leaders in the gospel of Christ and refuse to allow skin colour to play a part in their ministries

My friends, colleagues and close ones who inspired me and encouraged me through the lonely walk of writing

My beloved brother Last Arthur Nhema who God called to His heavenly home soon after I had just completed this book. Any time earlier could have significantly altered my mood and focus in writing.

TABLE OF CONTENTS

PREFACE

I listened to the voice of one of Africa's greatest man of God as he roused the multitudes to share the vision he has for Africa. He sang:

"Coming down, down, down,
Coming down
The glory of the Lord is coming down
When the saints begin to pray
For the Lord to have His way
Then the glory of the Lord is coming down!"

He and many other great men of God stand out as princes who rise from the land of Ham and stand in the gap for their people. They speak words of comfort to the weeping motherland of black people and believe in an Africa filled with the glory of the Lord. They have a vision of an Africa that can once again grow confident and raise hands with the world to say, "Yes, we can in Jesus' name!" For the psalmist prophesied, "Ethiopia (land of black people) shall soon stretch out her hands unto God."(Psalms 68:31) And when that happens, there is nothing that her children can't do or can't be.

Why are crime, deprivation, famine, misfortune and suffering often identified with a black person's face? Does God love black people the same way He seems to love other ethnic groups? If He does, what proof if any, does the bible have of this love?

This is a gentle but hard-hitting book on the role of black people in the bible. It is prayerfully hoped to motivate my fellow black people to comprehend the bible and to be blessed with a new confidence of the very important role God has for them in His purpose. This book is out to prove that it is because of the great love story between black people and God that the devil has unleashed endless wrath upon Africa and her children all over the world. And in this love lies the blessing that Africa should learn to receive. The blessing that bears the power to destroy the curses on her children!

Written by a serious intercessor who has personal experiences of living with the curse mentality inherited from colonialism and many years of flirtation with Darwin's evolutionary teachings, this book is based on prayerful research of the bible's 66 books over 30 years as a Christian. When God told me in 2006 to read the bible Chapters 1-11 of Genesis and gave me the name 'Seth' (Eve's third son) as a starting point, little did I know that after my many years of reading the bible and other books, a new understanding and knowledge of God's word was ready to be expressed. A young prayerful African Christian mother and colleague kept asking my advice about curses and blessings and in almost 'accidental' research, I 'stumbled' upon the central theme of blessings and curses on which the whole bible story is based. She has never known how her inquisitive spirit inspired revelation into deep secrets of the bible. This book is also based on a lot of reading from other Christians and non-Christians, though no formal references may have been found necessary of most widely held and biblically-supported views I have used. My strong personal opinions, backed by a passion for my black ancestry, has made this work an expression of the basic questions that simple black Christians like me ask every day.

I wrote this book from a layman's perspective, with as little biblical jargon as possible. I have discovered that events that happened in the bible mirror events that happened and still happen to nations and individuals. Therefore I have used this licence to interpret some issues around the descendants of Ham. It is my prayer that the simplicity of this book will help the reader to love the bible and to comprehend it in a deeper and more personal way. Welcome to a love story that I discovered hidden in the pages of the bible.

*Apologies: From the start I would like to apologise for what may appear like insensitive statements made about non-black people in this book. This book is targeted at black people who are trying to make sense of their blackness and role in the bible. In no way does this demean the tremendous role that non-black individuals played and continue to play in the lives of black people and the kingdom of God. Ideally, the gospel of Christ is about a kingdom where race and colour need not to be mentioned. Unfortunately, we black Christians daily find ourselves dealing with cases where colour is an issue inside and outside the body of Christ and often want to express our feelings without feeling guilty about doing so. This book is intended to identify with the ordinary black person's questions and to stir black people to love themselves and others through their comprehension of God's love written in many pages of the bible. As a black Christian I feel that this awareness is desperately lacking in many books I have read and messages I have heard.

There are books written by black authors for black people which often leave one feeling more wretched and hopeless after reading them. Written often from an analytical angle, they tend to give the diagnosis for black people's problems but lack the importance of faith in a God of love and purpose as the sure prescription for these problems.

*I would also like to acknowledge many writers and activists who share the vision of the resurgence of African might and who propose other methods to see it fulfilled. While I respect their views and achievements, I have dedicated this book only to the role of the biblical method in bringing change to Africa and her black children. As a devout Christian, this is my conviction, drive and prayerful approach to this question.

*While the focus of this book is Africa and her children and their role in God's plan for man, opportunity has been taken to share some deep secrets that God has personally revealed to me about particular issues in His word. I thank the Lord that He has answered some of my questions in the bible by leading me to sources of answers in my reading but more so by giving me exceptional revelation of His word. If I can help someone to know more about God through the story of the black bride, my humble duty would have been done. As a gifted writer, my talent would have been used to His glory.

Options in reading this book

Option1: For those who want the passionate appeal to the role of black people in the bible I recommend reading Chapters 1, 2, 4, 10, 11, 12, 13, 14.

Option 2: For those who want both the passionate appeal and to explore other biblical topics related to the role of black people in the bible I recommend reading the book just as it is.

Option 3: For those who want more scriptural evidence plus subjective views linked to this book I recommend reading the book as it is together with or followed by the Chapters under NOTES. Five Chapters of supporting notes have also been added to help with further reading material. These NOTES are optional reading material.

*Finally I strongly urge readers to keep the King James Version bible open as they will need to look up scriptures quoted or referred to.

Chapter 1
Introducing the age-old controversy of the children of Noah

The three sons of Noah namely Shem, Ham and Japheth were chosen by God as the patriarchs of all nations that were to populate the earth. Together with their father they had partaken in the divine story of salvation from the Flood and were specifically blessed by God Himself with a new covenant beneath the testimony of the rainbow (Genesis 9:1). As patriarchs, they were endued with God's power to build nations and to determine the world's three basic skin colours and those body features that God had in mind for the different nations. Each of them also appears to have had in them and their descendants an image of the coming Saviour, as we shall see later.

Only Japheth and Shem were blessed by Noah (Gen. 9:26-27). The world today is dominated by Japheth's descendants (Caucasians and Orientals). The glory of humanity is testimony of God's greater glory and of His wisdom which he shares with His creation. Japhethic nations appear to lead in promoting this glory, and preparing the world for the greater glory of Christ's rule. Christ's future kingdom is a highly advanced kingdom with only bits of its taste shared with our developed world today.

Salvation to man came through Shem's descendants. The chosen Shemitic group of the Hebrews was entrusted with God's plan for salvation. God's faithfulness to save man is represented by Shem. Christianity, Judaism, Islam and Hinduism are the biggest religions in the world, mostly pioneered by Shem's descendants. Most of the Christ-denying faiths are like the Phillistine wheat fields, ready and waiting for God's 'Samsons' to loose the foxes with their burning tails into their midst (Judges 15). This fire will awaken a new hunger for the true Bread of heaven and unprecedented revival of souls into the kingdom of God and His Christ. Through Shem man's hungry search for God shall be satisfied.

What image of Christ does Ham and his descendants bear? The curse came by Ham's family. Servanthood was his son, Canaan's reward. Ham was denied a father's blessing by Noah for seeing him naked. Ham's descendants have suffered more curses and abuse than any other group of Noah's descendants.

Though they share Japheth's glory and Shem's salvation, Ham's descendants appear to bear the image of the cross on their shoulder for which God chose one from their land, Simon of Cyrene (Libya), to carry up the Golgotha hill. They seem to be identified with the suffering image of their Saviour who bore the curse of His people and became servant of servants like Canaan the cursed son of Ham. To comprehend the despised role that the Saviour endured, one has to look at the suffering and despised role of many of Ham's children in the world today. This image has made them the object of so much controversy today like Jesus. But just as the Saviour's humble role became His ascend to glory, so is there so much hope for the humble descendants of Ham and so many who suffer like them of sharing in the glory of their Saviour.

However, the often misunderstood role of Ham in the bible and the world today has continued to subject his children to endless debate and scorn. One often comes across a lot of judgements passed on Ham and his descendants which are very difficult to justify. Several prophecies in the bible on Hamitic nations are used by some to explain why the nations of the children of Ham have not developed like other people. I have read some books that make the oppressors of Ham's children in all generations feel justified in doing what they did. When scriptures of judgement on Ham's children are quoted so freely, one could get the impression that no other nation in the world committed crimes worse than those of black people. Not many writers point at accountability on the part of the nations that carried out God's supposed judgement on Ham's children.

God uses the law of accountability. He shows this when He warned Assyria of her own judgement for fulfilling His punishment on rebellious Israel. In Isaiah 10:12-13 God warns Assyria that, "Wherefore it shall come to pass, that when the Lord has performed his whole work upon mount Zion and on Jerusalem, I will punish the fruit of the stout heart of the king of Assyria, and the glory of his high looks. For he saith, By the strength of my hand I have done it, and by my wisdom; for I am prudent and I have removed the bounds of the people, and have robbed their treasures, and I have put down the inhabitants like a valiant man."

Nations used by God to punish other nations do not do so on a crusade for the Lord. It is not as if they hear God's word instructing them to punish other nations. They do it for their own selfish and conceited reasons, giving themselves praise for it, while inadvertently fulfilling His will. Many who came to rob Africa of her children and resources may have actually done so on the instructions of the devil. When nations came to enslave Africa's children, they may have stumbled on some scripture to silence their conscience: but they did it for commercial greed. It is often easy to find scripture that could justify this crime but often the accountability and subsequent judgement of these punishers is not highlighted. Revelations 13:10 states a timeless law of God's judgement, "He that leadeth into captivity shall go into captivity; he that killeth with the sword must be killed with the sword. Here is the patience and the faith of the saints."

This principle of God's retribution is directed at the last kingdom of man headed by the antichrist, but can be applied to crimes that nations commit against other nations. However, quite often when judgement befalls the punisher, less discerning eyes may miss it. There is no nation clever enough to escape judgement for its sins. Often, people living through one generation may be mistaken when judgement does not befall their oppressors in their lifetime. This feeling was also common among the early church Christians who were persecuted by Rome. Some of their persecutors outlived many of them. That is why God advises patience to His saints. Even an open door into the afterlife shows the souls of dead saints pleading with God for vengeance (Revelations 6:9-11). God works at His own timetable and we are admonished to wait patiently for His unfailing justice.

There are those who propose that slavery and colonialism in Africa was judgement for Egypt's enslavement of Jews around 1400 BC. I would respectfully beg to differ. Why judgement had to wait for generations 3000 years after the enslavement is not very convincing. When will the crimes committed by the generations in between be judged? If God will only judge those crimes written in the bible, then the bible ceases to be a witness to every generation. The bible is not a closed book but an open witness of how God deals with nations and individuals. In every generation different nations and different people commit crimes and sin that attract judgement in their generation.

Though the bible record shows God's dealing mainly with Shemitic and Hamitic nations, it is obvious that according to His nature, He was blessing and judging other nations not named in the bible in the same manner. Japheth's descendants are not mentioned much in the bible story but that does not mean that they were beyond God's reach. For example judgement on the

Japhethic nations in league with Persia(Iran) in Ezekiel 38 and 39 is frightening levels of judgement in waiting. The fearsome way by which God will miraculously intervene to save Israel from these nations will leave the world without a doubt that He is alive and strong. It looks like Japhethic nations have been reserved as testimony of God's power over man's most powerful and glorious kingdoms. The way God is going to engage the superpowers of this world will be a testimony of His awesome power and presence. The fear of the Lord will shake the whole world when God judges Japhethic nations.

God also uses the law of proportion in judgement. It would be against His character in His word not to. Many questions come to mind because of this law. If Ham should be punished for seeing his father Noah's nakedness, how much shall be the punishment of those who stripped naked the Son of God and nailed Him? If Egypt shall be punished for enslaving Israel how much shall those who killed 6million Jews in the holocaust be punished? What was/will be the punishment of those who carried millions of black people into slavery subjecting them to unimaginable suffering? If slavery and subjugation of black people was punishment for the sin of Ham, were the traumatic World Wars a punishment for any particular people's sins? And which people? If the land of Ham is still being punished for robbing Solomon's Temple when will the punishment for the AD 70 destruction of the Temple start? And when will the punishment of the nations who have continued to treat Israel like their own colony begin? Or of those who continue to rob Africa of her resources? These are some of the questions that those who seek to apportion judgement on Ham's children have to answer. Picking on a weakened continent like Africa and her problems to show God's judgement seems to suggest that God is incapable of judging powerful nations! He definitely isn't. As God's grace for the good deeds of the forefathers wears thin because of a godless generation of sons and daughters who have been born to peace and security, judgement will follow.

We also have to deal with God's law on the lifespan of parental sins. In Exodus 20:5 He says that He visits the iniquity of the fathers on their children only as far as the third and fourth generations. If 100 years could be the maximum of a biblical generation, then Ham's iniquity is more than forty generations ago. Why should it be punished more than four generations later? God foretold that Abraham's descendants would possess the land of Canaan in the fourth generation after the curse of the Canaanites would have peaked (Genesis 15:16). This confirms with the principle of fourth generation visitation of iniquity that God refers to in Exodus 20.The sins of Ham's children against Israel and recorded in the bible are more than 20 generations ago. In Ezekiel 18 God went a step further to say that children would not be punished for the sins of their fathers but that the soul that sinned would be responsible for its sins. This links well with the new covenant in Christ which nailed all the generational handwriting of families' sins and curses to the cross (Colossians 2:14).

Jesus came to bear the guilt of nations. Most judgements on nations written in the bible have already been fulfilled unless the prophecy specifically says they are not. They remain complete testimonies of God's warning to nations and individuals alike warning them of God's ways. While some learned behaviours from cursed predecessors often continue to shape the lifestyles of future generations, it is up to Ham's children who now know the Lord to set up standards of a God-fearing lifestyle for their land and for future generations. I believe this is the reason why the Psalmist prophesies specifically about princes coming out of Egypt in Psalms 68. Princes of the kingdom of heaven are needed in the land of Ham to give a new royal code of a lifestyle pleasing to God.

This book is dedicated to repudiating the blame and curse teaching that generations of well-meaning and not-so well-meaning teachers have heaped on Ham's descendants. If anything, most of the problems of Ham's children are man-made by devil-inspired people who twisted scripture and misused science to justify their greed. This blame has weighed so heavily on the minds of Ham's descendants that, together with other racially driven views, the burden is very hard for them to bear.

Ham's children's have suffered a lot of guilt and blame over the ages that what they yearn to hear is the voice of love and comfort. I believe that they yearn to hear their Saviour saying, "Come unto me all ye that labour and are heavy laden, and I will give you rest,"(Matthew 11:28) and to hear the Bridegroom whispering to them, "Rise up, my love, my fair one, and come away. For, lo, the winter is past, the rain is over and gone," (Song of Solomon 2:10-11).They yearn for the Blessing that will set them free from the curse of the devil and of man.

Chapter 2
"The land of Ham" Psalms 106:22

The 'land of Ham' named here is the land of Egypt founded by one of Ham's sons. Ham and his two brothers Shem and Japheth lived in Mesopotamia and probably died there while their sons spread out over the earth. The probability of old Ham migrating with one of his sons is not farfetched but God's reduction of man's life by decree just before the Flood(Genesis 6:3) may suggest that Ham and his brothers died before migration from the aborted tower of Babel. Therefore reference to Egypt as the land of Ham could be because many of Ham's descendants settled in this continent where Egypt was the most powerful of them.

Ham had four sons, namely Canaan, Mizraim, Cush and Phut. While Canaan settled in the present land of Israel and near Middle East, the rest of his brothers' descendants are mainly found in Africa. Mizraim settled in Egypt and his children are featured more than the rest of Ham's sons in the bible. Cush was the original founder of some of Mesopotamia's major cities while some of his sons moved and populated a large area from Saudi Arabia, Yemen to East Africa generally known by the Greek name Ethiopia which means land of dark-skinned people.

By the time the bible was written and concluded, the land of Africa was known as the land of Cush/ Egypt /Ethiopia. Africa is a more recent name to the continent. This land, featuring so much in the bible, was and has remained the land of dark-skinned people in all their beautiful and diverse shades of dark skin (See Notes Chapter 5 for further reading).

It is generally accepted that the Song of Solomon and his many brides in Jerusalem was a shadow of the eternal Bridegroom and Lover, Jesus Christ and His wise virgins from all nations of the world, echoing through spiritual Jerusalem. Of special interest in this book is the virgin/bride who describes herself as 'black but comely' (1:5).

The black bride of the heavenly Solomon (Jesus Christ) describes herself with the characteristic features of a beautiful virgin from the land of the descendants of Ham. There is no good reason to dispute this. It appears like the Lord had a long affair with the land of Ham and makes this obvious in this beautiful love song. We will retrace the story of this lengthy affair.

Ham is on record for not covering his father, Noah's nakedness when he found him thus intoxicated in his tent. Nowhere does the bible say or suggest that Ham laughed at his father's nakedness. It simply states that he left him uncovered and told it to his two brothers who did the more honourable act of covering their father's nakedness.

However, besides his reckless and dishonourable behaviour to his father's nakedness, Ham has never ceased to amaze in the bible. Though he did not receive the father's blessing that Noah gave his other two sons, Ham seemed to have excelled on the blessing he had received from God the day the family left the ark(Genesis 9:1). It is quite clear that Ham was the nation founder and builder in the bible. His son Cush was the father of the great Nimrod, founder of the cities of Babel, Calneh, Erech and Accad. Cush is by his name identified as darker-skinned than his brothers. It is not unusual in dark-skinned children to find some darker than the rest.

Another of the Cushites , Asshur, founded Nineveh and four other cities. Asshur was the forefather of the powerful Assyrians. The Assyrians who featured so much in the bible story are traced to Ham. The Middle East was founded by the children of Ham including the Babylonian kingdom. Some of Cush's descendants remained around the Babylonian area and intermarried with Shem's and Japheth's descendants leading to the many shades of colours found in that part of the world today.

Ham's son Mizraim was the founder and builder of the Egyptian kingdom, one of the most advanced founder kingdoms in the world who invented shaduf irrigation, the 365 day calendar and the weaving of cloth from cotton. Their architectural skills have remained a wonder to the world. The mathematical precision in the construction of their pyramids remains a present day puzzle to modern scholars.

Canaan founded the land of Canaan that would one day be known as the land of milk and honey. This land has become the focus of the whole world as the Holy Land where the Saviour was born, bred and died and arose for the salvation of the whole world. Canaan's sons built Jerusalem, Tyre, Sidon and the legendary traders the Phoenicians are descended from him. It is utterly false and unbiblical to call the Canaanites Shemites. They were Hamites though it is unknown how much they resembled or differed from the original looks of Shemites . Intermarriage over many years may also have led to the semitic looks. The exceptional civilisation of Tyrus that the bible describes in great detail in Ezekiel 26, 27 and 28 can be compared to the legend of Atlantis that nations believe sank into the sea. Tyrus was overtaken by Satan himself leading to God's judgement on her. This city has remained almost apocalyptic in prophecy.

Phut founded Lybia and the North African countries. Cush's other sons founded the land of Ethiopia in East Africa, south of the Nile (Sudan) and lands beyond the rivers of Ethiopia (Isaiah 18) which must refer to other inner African states.

God chose to weave the bible story around these lands founded by the descendants of Ham and as we shall see, built the nation of Israel with or around the children of Ham. That in itself should be accounted for honour to Ham. Ham is used by God to lay the stage on which the heavenly story was played and he remained an active actor in the story. On his descendant's shoulder would the cross be laid as Christ laid the foundation of the kingdom of heaven. We will briefly trace how this develops.

God chooses Abraham from a Shemite family and calls him out of the Babylonian city of Ur, gives him a unique covenant of blessings and sends him to live as a stranger in the land of Canaan. He interacts with the Canaanite tribes to a God-agreed level. Though his cousin Lot gets vexed by the evil lifestyle of one of the Canaanite cities of Sodom, God ensured that Abraham was enriched by his interaction with the Canaanites. He met Melchizedek, the priest of the most High God and king of Salem in Canaan. It is not known whether Melchizedek was a Canaanite. The bible is silent that he was not a Canaanite descendant either. His priestly genealogy is said to have been unknown (Genesis 14:18, Psalms 110:4, Hebrews 7).God shows His principle of grace to have the presence of this revered man as a resident of a land designated as a cursed land, just as He had other godly men like Job in Uz and possibly others in other nations spread out over the world who however did not have Melchizedek's unique office.

God sends Abraham down to Egypt; the first time He brings His chosen family from Shem's descendants into contact with the mainland of Ham. Though this contact was embarrassing for the children of Ham who God warned off Abraham's wife Sarah with great plagues, Pharaoh made amends with Abraham by compensating him with great wealth and servants. Ham's land will be remembered for providing Abraham a mother for his

Arab children in this unseemly manner. Sarah's maid, Hagar, must have been part of this compensation. Through her son Ishmael would rise a powerful nation of 12 sons blessed with the wealth of the wells of the desert oil. The Canaanite king Abimelech also adds to Abraham's wealth in similar fashion after embarrassing himself with his lust for Sarah as well. Abraham's clan and wealth grew in strength from his interaction with Ham's descendants. Another of Abimelech's princes also adds to Abraham's son Isaac's wealth by repeating the lust of his family on Rebekah and paying compensation at God's intervention.

The next significant interaction between Shem's children and Ham's children was when God made way for Joseph to become a slave in Egypt as His plan to prepare a nest for his chosen family of Israel in the land of Ham. In a significant move, God gave Jacob's dearest son to the land of Ham where he lifted the name of Egypt above all nations as the breadbasket of the world. Joseph has remained the role model to the land of Ham, who brought God's glory to the land. The blessing that followed Joseph was so powerful that Potiphar's home and business suddenly blossomed when he became their slave. Potiphar's wife must have identified Joseph as the source of this blessing and so desired it that she thought she could also share the anointing of the blessing by sleeping with him. The sad account of this denied request led to Joseph's imprisonment (Genesis 39). But the blessing was so powerful that it made Pharaoh dream prophetic dreams leading to Joseph assuming his destined role over the land of Ham. Joseph is the role model of young princes that the land of Ham should give birth to in order to bring about change to her land.

The warm relationship and peace that prevailed between Israel and Africa during Joseph's time remained a remembrance before God. The law of Moses stated that Israel should not hate the Egyptian and that their third generation of children should be allowed access into Lord's assembly (Deuteronomy 23:8). Joseph married Asnath, the daughter of an Egyptian priest and two of their sons became Jacob's sons by adoption and were allocated inheritance in Israel as the tribes of Ephraim and Manasseh. From Ephraim's tribe God chose Joshua to take over from Moses and lead the children of Israel into Canaan.

The most significant of God's continuing testimony of his love for the land of Ham is obviously the baby King Jesus' abode in Egypt. After several centuries during which Egypt had fought on the sides of God's enemies, ransacked the first temple of Jerusalem and after prophets had made serious prophetic warnings against the land of Egypt, one would have expected God to have nothing more to do with it. But God still chose the land of Ham to protect His Son and the children of Ham still welcomed exiles like they had done when Israel went into Egypt. The Old covenant had identified Africa with the title of "the house of bondage," which is synonymous with evil. Before the New covenant could be written, God altered that image. After His Son's asylum in Egypt, Africa has become associated with land of asylum from which God called His Son. It is also probable that the rise of another 'Herod'/antichrist in future will force many children of Israel to follow the example of Jesus down to Africa and into her deserts seeking asylum.

The interaction between Israel and either the descendants of Ham by Canaan, Mizraim or Cush is also traced through many examples like Moses' Ethiopian/Medianite wife, Joseph's Egyptian wife and mother of the tribes of Ephraim and Manasseh. The genealogy line of Christ also runs through Canaanite parentage of Rahab the prostitute of Jericho, while it is not clear whether David's wife Bathsheba was Hittite, or not, like her former husband Uriah the Hittite. She was the mother of Solomon from whose parentage Christ is traced. Other significant involvement of Ham's descendants in the bible story involves individuals like Cushi the messenger of king David, the queen of Sheba, Hiram the king of Tyre and architect of Solomon's Temple, Ebed-Melech the Ethiopian eunuch who saved prophet Jeremiah from the dungeon, Zephaniah the prophet, Simon the Canaanite disciple of Jesus, Simon of Cyrene who bore Christ's cross, the father of Alexander and Rufus, Simeon called Niger and the Ethiopian eunuch.

The issue of the role of dark-skinned people in the bible has significantly irritated other nations who feel that they should have been more represented in the bible story. A lot of jealousy and misgiving has driven some writers to pick needles in haystacks just to try and prove that the bible does not mean what it actually says. Some of the exaggerated interest in Egyptian mummies is partly driven by abortive attempts to prove that the early Egyptians were not dark-skinned people. Attempts have also been made to try and deny most Africans descent from Cush, the son of Ham by classifying them as Negroes of no traceable ancestry. But the argument gets unstuck when some of the early disciples in Acts of the Apostles included names like Niger which are very closely related to Niger and Nigeria today. God did a compact job in the writing of the bible. Even the most rabid blogger cannot disprove that God gave Ham an outstanding role in the bible story. And typical with God's nature, He has a significant role for Ham to play in the future of the story of mankind. It is God's law of the past, present and future that, "That which hath been is now; and that which is to be hath already been; and God requireth that which is past."

(Ecclesiastes 3:15.)

The events that happened at Calvary confirm God's remembrance for the land of Ham. The fact that three lands were represented at the cross is not just mere coincidence. The land of Shem was represented by the jeering Jews, the land of Japheth by the ruthless Romans and the land of Ham by Simon of Cyrene (Libya) in North Africa. The Romans would not dare to compel a Jew awaiting to partake of Passover to carry the cross of Jesus and therefore picked on this African inhabitant who Mark says had just arrived this way from the countryside. It has remained an unsung honour for Africa to bear the cross of Christ. Simon did not share the guilt of wilful participation in the death of Christ. The land of Ham was vindicated in this man. Could the indignity of Ham's reckless behaviour towards Noah years ago have been revisited with honour on this day? I believe this was God's sign that it had.

Jesus, the Lord of the Sabbath, hung at Calvary on the sixth day of man's labour. He was laid to rest at the start of the Sabbath and rested in the grave throughout the seventh day. The Creator Himself and the earth He created rested together on the seventh day in a significant union. The earth, cursed at Adam's fall with hard labour, was now blessed with the Giver of rest and blessings in her womb. He was the Rest/ Sabbath that man had waited for and which the Sabbath had signified all these years. In Him all man's labour and debts were dead and buried. When He resurrected on the first day of a new week He gave man a new Covenant of rest in His finished sacrifice and trust in Him. In this new covenant God had forgiven the debts and sin of past generations and saw them nailed on the cross and buried with His Son. If Ham indeed remained indebted to his father after so many generations and if Egypt remained indebted to the Lord for troubling Israel over the years, including by helping Israel's enemies fight the kingdoms of Israel, then indeed, this was the Man on whom every debt of mankind was paid. Indeed Jesus was the Jubilee of God to set every captive free, both the redeemed robber on the cross and the unredeemed robber Barabbas!

God's love for Africa continued to be seen after the 12 apostles had taken over the reins of the kingdom. God had a messenger for Ethiopia (Acts 8). As stated above, Ethiopia is Greek name for land of dark-skinned people beyond the south of the Nile River while the name Sudan is the Arabic word for the same land. The Candace was the black queen of Ethiopia/Sudan. It is quite obvious that to allow her chief eunuch time to worship God at Jerusalem showed how strongly she must have felt about the God of Israel. She must have been very thrilled when her eunuch returned with a new revelation of

God that evangelist Phillip had been sent to minister to him. The Holy Spirit had underlined the enormity of this encounter by the wonder of literally lifting Phillip. The Holy Spirit had a message for Ethiopia and it had to be delivered.

Is it reasonable to believe that the eunuch became an evangelist where he went? It is also reasonable to assume that the eunuch continued visiting the disciples in Jerusalem and that they may have sent some teachers of the gospel with him to support his work in Ethiopia. There is an obvious unwritten story of missionary activity in Africa from Ethiopia by the eunuch and from North Africa by Simon of Cyrene. Both had had a mighty visitation of God's remembrance. It is sad that with all this love of God reaching out to her, the land of Ham seems to have been careless with keeping the fire burning. Together with Shem, Ham slowly drifted out of the missionary picture which Japheth embraced and enlarged.

However, a resurgence of the role of the church (bride) from the land of black people is now overtaking many nations with giant strides. The unfulfilled love journey between Christ and His black bride which is so powerful in her that she cries out, "I charge you O daughters of Jerusalem, if you find my beloved, that ye tell him, that I am sick of love," (Song of Solomon 5:8) is back on the world stage. Just as unconsummated love makes one sick, the black bride is embracing her lost and True Lover and will not let go of Him again. Before this love song can be heard, let us retrace the footsteps of Ham's children back into the cradle of the divine plan of blessings. (As for further reading on the love of God please proceed to Notes Chapter 1.)

Chapter 3
Curses and blessings

Introduced by one of the most credible storytellers ever known to men, in the name of Moses, the genesis/beginning of the story of God and man shows the picture of a God who, like a Master Carpenter, chisels away all the rough edges of the building and out of chaos calls forth light. There is no other record of a man who spent more time than Moses in the presence of God. He had all the time to ask the questions and to get the right answers from God Himself. Anyone who prayerfully reads the creation story will be impressed by how it links so masterfully with the whole bible story.

God makes the first covenant with Adam. Then He makes the second covenant with Noah and his sons below the rainbow. The third covenant is with Abraham under the night stars. The fourth covenant witnessed by the blood of the Lamb was with His own Son who reconciled all the covenants in Himself. That is why Christ is called the last Adam. God so respected His covenant with Adam in the Garden that He was prepared to walk on earth in the image of fallen man to redeem it. The first Adam was created in the image of God while the last Adam was God Himself come down to earth to reconcile all things unto Himself. The story of man in the bible is the story of parallels, the image of that which is cursed and that which is blessed.

By choosing the tree of knowledge of good and evil the first Adam chose life with curses. Parallel to the tree of knowledge of good and evil was the Tree of life representing Jesus Christ the last Adam. The Old testament/covenant is the record of the story of Adam's children struggling to be like God by laws of good and evil and bloodshed of animals. Parallel to the Old covenant follows the New covenant/testament written about the last Adam giving life to man to become children of God and renewed with the blessing that God had purposed for man in Eden.

The parallels run through Adam's family with Cain going the way of the curse and Abel the way of the blessing. The pattern repeats itself in Noah's family, Abraham's family, Isaac's family and Jacob's divided family. The children of Adam then become divided into two parallel groups of Gentiles and Israelites. The Gentiles uphold the parallel city founded on the curse called Babylon (see below) while the chosen people of Israel uphold the symbol of blessing, the city of Jerusalem. The last Adam reconciles the parallels, Gentiles and Israelites, by His blood. But the world still continues to pursue a choice of parallels. The wide road leads to the pleasures of Babylon and through its gate to eternal damnation in hell, while the narrow path leads through Jerusalem to eternal blessing in heaven.

It is important to remember that when Adam fell in Eden, he gave the serpent a claim in his line of descendants. The devil would lay claim to Adam's descendants and exercise the right to influence a part of his descendants. From the first two families recorded in the bible, the devil laid claim to one of them. He claimed Cain in Adam's family and laid claim to Ham's son in Noah's family. Unless God's grace had shielded Ham's entire heritage, the devil could have used Noah's wrath to hold claim to entire nations descended from Ham. Noah could not curse one that God had blessed. God had blessed Ham too beneath the rainbow the day they came out of the ark (Genesis 9:1).All the same, it is important to grasp the fact that in all family accounts recorded in the bible and those not recorded, wherever a blessing was, the curse was also there. This imperfection of God's creation after Adam's fall would require only the blood of the creator Himself to heal it.

God's business is to bless His creation which He loved and called good after He created it (Genesis 1). Satan's business is to curse God's beautiful creation and make God's plan for man fail. But curses have a limited lifespan (Exodus 20:5) because God would not allow an eternal curse on a fallible humanity. God also ensured that He rid Adam's descendants of the curse of Cain by ensuring that all of Cain's descendants perished in the Flood. Noah's surviving family had descended from Adam's third and righteous son Seth who Eve had named as replacement for her slain son Abel (Genesis 4:25). The reduction of human lifespan was another of God's way of ensuring that curses and sins would also die with them. Only blessings bear eternal life. (For more information on Cain and his descendants refer to Notes).

God used individuals that He chose to ensure that blessings continued to be available to man. Noah, Abraham, Isaac, Jacob were made patriarchs of these blessings. Whoever they blessed God blessed. The whole bible story is full of blessings that God allowed other servants of His to bless individuals and nations because God's plan for man is based on the flow of blessings. Jesus is the sum of the blessing of God to the world and to man. And in similar fashion He has instructed us to bless and not curse. When we bless we are exercising God's nature.

Noah blessed his two sons Shem and Japheth. The blessings have remained with them to this day. Shem was given the blessing to be the custodian of salvation to this world. Out of Shem came the Hebrew group of Abraham's children, from whom the line of Christ originates. The four largest religions in the world today have originated from the family of Shem. Japheth was given the blessing to be enlarged and the record of his sons was greater than others'. Most of today's powerful kingdoms come from Japheth's children. He also appears to have been blessed with the role of enlarging the world's capacity but instructed to dwell under the tent of Shem. Japheth's blessing was limited to his acknowledgement of the God of Shem.

However, it is obvious that some families of Japheth have fulfilled this role and taken a leading role in enlarging the tent of Shem's God (Isaiah 54:2) which Shem had limited by his denial of Christ. No one can deny that Japheth's children have also enlarged civilisations in the world, improved on previous inventions and ideas and preserved knowledge. But this role could all go wrong the day they step out of the tent of Shem.

Though Ham did not receive a father's blessing He excelled on God's blessing on his life (Genesis 9:1) to become the builder of nations. Ham laid the foundation of the nations where the salvation story would be written by Shem. He founded the nations of Babylon, Assyria, Nineveh, Canaan, Egypt/Ethiopia. God ensured that a blessing followed Ham's children by sending patriarchs with blessings after them. His plan for the salvation of man depended on the principle of blessing.

Abraham blessed Ham's land by his presence in Egypt and peaceful settlement of compensation for Sarah. The blessing also passed onto Hagar's children in the process. Jacob blessed Pharaoh (Genesis 47:10) in Egypt fulfilling the patriarch blessing on the land of Ham. The land of Ham welcomed Joseph and revered Jacob with the respect reserved for their father. They mourned him for 70 days and when they went for his funeral, their grievous funeral mourning for him beyond the Jordan was renowned as Abel-Mizraim (Genesis 50:11).God has not forgotten the voices of the children of Ham weeping beyond the river of Jordan.

God's ultimate blessing for the land of Ham was the sending of His Son Baby Jesus to find refuge there. It was a confirmation of his love and blessing for Ham and an honour many nations would have preferred was their own. This honour should not be downplayed just because it happened to Africa. For here was One, greater than Noah, the Blessing in human form, come to visit the land of Ham.

By comparison, when newly pregnant Mary visited Elizabeth's home, the foetus John jumped for joy in His mother's womb at the arrival of the awesome Seed in Mary's womb and Elizabeth began to prophesy. In the same way must have the princes awaiting their birth leapt in joy in the womb of their old and wrinkled motherland of Africa when the Baby Jesus Christ descended on Africa. She who the world has called barren of princes shall come out of hiding and prophesy. She shall see the decree of Mary fulfilled on her own people too, "He hath shown strength with his arm; he hath scattered the proud in the imagination of their hearts. He hath put down the mighty from their seats, and exalted them of low degree. He hath filled the hungry with good things; and the rich he hath sent away empty."(Luke 1:51-53) Mary prophesied of a time when starting with the poor in Israel, a new order of blessings would upset the classes of man. Even those in Africa who the proud world had classified as undeserving of the resources, pleasures and comforts of this world others deemed more deserving can have, were by God's powerful Blessing called Jesus Christ, given access to a more powerful heavenly resource treasure that the deserving could not access.

Over the ages, God has kept His love and blessing reaching out to earth. By ensuring almost perfect laws of nature, He has assured man of a stable world to plan their lives. He has also used judgement to destroy curses that would severely contaminate man. The destruction of Sodom is a perfect example of this. Those who must have known of these cities must have gone spreading the word everywhere, about the judgement of God on evil nations. It served as a warning to other people of the day as it does to people today that God will not tolerate heinous God-defying lifestyles. However, God had been ready to spare these cities if only five righteous people had been found in it. That's how longsuffering God is. Those who do not understand this quality of His may end up in bitterness like Jonah. He wanted God to destroy Nineveh for their enslaving of Israel's tribes but was shocked that God had a different plan. God loved and wanted to bless Nineveh if they repented. This is similar to God advising the Jews going into exile to Babylon to pray for the peace of their city of exile.

The children of Israel have been dispersed all over the world. Their genes are found in many groups of people in the world, sometimes down to the remotest village in Africa. They also seem to have carried the twelve blessings of their tribes all over the world in the process. This could have been part of God's plan to spread the blessing to all nations. This pattern is repeated when persecution dispersed the disciples all over the world to spread the blessing of salvation. God still disperses Christians all over the world to do the same. And Africa has been the focus of this dispersion in recent times. Whosoever bears the word of God carries a blessing

God jealously guards the blessing that He gives. This is evident when He resisted the diviner Balaam from pronouncing a curse on Israel (Numbers 22). While it is not clear what the curse could have altered of the strong blessing of Israel, the curious involvement of Moab, the descendants of Lot in the plan of the curse could have got God involved the way He did. This was the land of Lot's descendants close to the river Jabbok where Jacob had wrestled an angelic being many years back. Besides his sad account in the bible, Lot had shared in God's blessing for Abraham. His descendants shared part of that blessing. A paradox of two nations' destinies seems to have presented itself here. Balaam encountered a resisting angel and ended up blessing Jacob's descendants instead of cursing them. God appears to have remembered Jacob's wrestling contest with the angel and allowed his children to wrestle a blessing from this contest too.

This awareness will give aggrieved people a sober reflection of human limit in God's purpose. God's purpose is driven by His faithfulness to covenant, His love and His mercy. Man's sin is the one that triggers judgement on them. Throughout the bible God makes it clear that He will withhold judgement if righteous people intercede on behalf of others. He also sustains nations that have received blessings because His purpose flows on rivers of blessing to diffuse curses. Further ahead we shall see how God turns the curse of Noah on Canaan into a blessing for the whole world.

Kingdom of man and kingdom of God

It is quite easy to be misled by both spiritual and political emotions of the church and media to think that as Christians we can pray our will to alter God's will. There are two kingdoms in the affairs of the descendants of Adam. The first is called the kingdom of man while the second is called the kingdom of God and His Christ. Both kingdoms need to give birth to princes who can be entrusted with the qualities needed to run just government in every nation. When individuals without God-endowed princely qualities rule in man's kingdoms, the nations are cursed with endless problems. When individuals without the new birth experiences to be sons/princes of God run governments/ministry in the Kingdom of God, the Kingdom is in danger of captivity.

God has chosen Israel as His inheritance in the kingdom of man. We cannot pray to have that changed. This gives them special favour and an elect status in this world. It does not matter how small Israel may look, but what happens in Israel affects all nations of the kingdom of man. Therefore those who know their God cannot leave Israel out of their prayers if they hope for peace, justice and prosperity in the kingdom of man. However this elect status of Israel in itself does not give them eternal favour or automatic right into the Kingdom of God and His Christ which they can only get if and when they accept Jesus and get born-again like everyone else. That's why it was important that the statement of the need to be born again was first made by Jesus to Nicodemus, a ruler in Israel (John 3:1-7). God has also made lesser covenants of blessings with the Arabic descendants of Ishmael, Esau and other sons of Abraham. We cannot change that. Yet like Israel and the rest of mankind they need to be born again to enter the Kingdom of God.

Moses gives revelation into God's number structure of the children of Adam. In Deuteronomy 32:8 he says, "When the Most High divided to the nations their inheritance, when he separated the sons of Adam, he set the bounds of the people according to the number of the children of Israel." He reveals that God has used Israel as the mirror in determining the inheritance of the nations descended from Adam.

The use of Israel as the mirror of God's plans with the world should have significant meaning. God divided Israel into 12 tribes. It is significant that God's blessing is spread out to the world through someone with the character of Jacob who identifies so much with the ordinary person's strengths and weaknesses! If the inheritance of Adam's children is mirrored by Israel then we can suggest that the world's nations sit on an architectural plan of 12 groups. How this is reflected on the world map divided by modern man may not be obvious. Maybe the original record of divisions during the days of Peleg, the great grandson of Shem (Genesis 10:25) when the first record of the division of the earth is mentioned, could have been by this number.

This pattern of the number 12 is repeated when the Kingdom of Christ is constructed on 12 disciples as well. This links well with the home of the redeemed in New Jerusalem which is founded on the number 12. (We know from Revelations that God's plan will be opposed by the devil who will build his cursed kingdom with his prince, the antichrist, on the foundation of the number 10 (ten toes of Daniel 2:41?) The number 12 suggests the perfect kingdom plan of God and pathway of His blessing. It is like the framework by which heaven and earth are linked in God's perfect will.

Going by the bible record, God has also chosen individual nations to lead the kingdom of man at different stages of history. The founding leading nations were from Ham viz Egypt/Ethiopia, Assyria and Nimrod's Babylon and Canaan. Various Shemitic nations have maintained their strong presence and bridged Ham's nations and Japhethic nations. These are the nations of Syria, Israel, Edom, Midian, Chaldean, Ishmaelites and Persia among the various groups in what is known as the Middle East including much of India.

The last leading nations are mainly from Japheth and emerged as Babylon of Medo-Persia, Greece and Rome. The Japhetic nations' dispensation as per the blessing and prophecy of Noah has been enlarged to include Caucasian nations in Asia, Americas and Australia. The shared power between Shem's nations and Japheth nations as prophesied by Noah is still apparent. Unlike Israel, they do not stand on the unchangeable covenant witnessed by Abraham, Isaac and Jacob. They have been given determined dispensation to exercise dominion. How they exercise that dominion will determine the curses and blessings they will reap. They have the choice to either strengthen themselves with the children of Israel or with other of Abraham's and Isaac's descendants. The opposing descendants of Abraham determine the balance of power in the kingdom of man to the end.

Those who know Christ cannot afford to ignore to bless the Lord God of Israel by which they have received the blessing of salvation. We also need to pray for the children of Abraham who the devil is ruthlessly engaging in killing one another. And whether we like the leading nations in this present world or not, God expects us to pray for them. In our prayers we need to be careful what we say because different nations have a paradox of blessings and curses in them. Not all the wealthy are wicked. Some are hardworking honest individuals or have inherited God's blessings on their righteous forefathers. Not all the poor are righteous. Some have inherited their due reward for their idleness, evil works and those of their parents.

The bible story is more about blessings than curses. It is testimony of the power of blessing over curses. There is more promise of God's love and forgiveness for all the children of Adam than about their damnation. In these pages we trace the footsteps of God's grace in the land of Ham and discover how God turns the curse of Noah on Ham's son Canaan into a blessing.

Chapter 4
The legendary curse of Ham

"Cursed be Canaan, a servant of servants shall he be…"
Genesis 9:25

This was the curse that was handed down on Ham's family, days after Noah had sobered from his embarrassing drunkenness and self-exposure to his sons. This does not sound like just an idle outburst of anger but rather a well thought-out disciplinary exercise. Noah's family must have grown to include grandchildren from his three sons Shem, Ham and Japheth. Whether the grandsons were married by that time, the bible does not say. The bible is also silent about the role of women in the whole episode but this was a family crisis that must not have escaped the women.

The patriarch and revered man of God, Noah, had been informed of how his son Ham had demeaned him in that after discovering him naked in the tent, he had not covered his nakedness but had proceeded to tell it to his two brothers. The grievous possibility could have seen Shem and Japheth sneaking into the tent and seeing their father's nakedness. Or just ignoring him to lie there naked like Ham did and a grandson could have also seen his nakedness. Nowhere in the text does it suggest that Ham mocked his father's nakedness. It simply says that Ham saw his father's nakedness and did not cover it, before telling it to his brothers who did the more honourable act of covering his nakedness with their backs turned to avoid seeing his nakedness. Ham's dishonourable and disrespectful behaviour could not go unpunished by the strong-willed patriarch who had in the recent past almost single-handedly defied the cynical world as he built the ark. He would have failed as a leader to condone such behaviour. The same God who blessed Noah's children would warn in His written statutes by Moses much later that children should respect their parents. This unwritten law must have been placed in the hearts of these patriarchs who were close to God.

Noah must have also remembered that day when God blessed him and his three sons (including Ham) after they left the ark. Genesis 9:1 states "And God blessed Noah and his sons, and said unto them, Be fruitful, and multiply, and replenish the earth." God was happy that, together with his sons, Noah had built the massive ark, engaged in the selection process of the living things that would go into the ark, fed the creatures and his sons had come out victorious and obedient to God's word to their father. Noah was obviously aware that God's blessing was powerful and could not be reversed. By these blessings on Noah's sons, God had bestowed on all the three sons of Noah the patriarchal roles over nations that would be descendant from them. This would be repeated hundreds of years later by Isaac who could not reverse his blessing on Jacob after Esau arrived (Genesis 27:33) and by the diviner Balaam who had significant knowledge of God and asked, "How shall I curse, whom God hath not cursed?" (Numbers 23:8). There was nothing Noah could do to reverse God's blessing on Ham. The only thing he could deny Ham was the father's blessing which he gave his two other sons. And Ham's disrespect of his father could also have invoked a shorter lifespan on his descendants as the law would state (Exodus 20:12).

But by choosing to discipline Ham through his last son Canaan, Noah knew that this would be a fitting semblance of discipline. Noah handed his guilty verdict on the unfortunate Canaan. Here was an example of the son receiving punishment for his father's faults. Generations later God would reject this kind of injustice by the mouth of His prophet in Ezekiel 18:17 stating that an innocent son would not die for the sins of his father.

By definition, the name Canaan is suggested to have referred to someone with good business skills. Whether Canaan was a very gifted business person as his name would imply or not, is not known. But the story of his descendants shows evidence of these skills. The Canaanite groups of nations in the land of Canaan itself and the Meditteranean sea areas in the later part of the Bible story were very skilled craftsmen. Normal human sentiment would suggest that a more telling curse would be felt by the recipient when it was directed at the best son. Very few fathers would be bothered if a curse was directed at their most useless sons. There must be a good reason why Canaan was picked out by Noah. And also a good reason why the Bible introduces the name Ham with reference to Canaan's name, "Ham, the father of Canaan.."(Genesis 9:18). There must have been something about Canaan that set him apart among Ham's sons. But nowhere in the bible does it suggest that Canaan was the father of black people of Africa. His descendants and their names are restricted to the lands near and around the east of the Meditteranean Sea.

Canaan must have been stung by this curse. He was also Noah's grandson and most grandfathers are close to their grandsons. Noah might have regretted drinking himself to this level of intoxication because the act itself had not been honourable. If anything, it had given occasion for a curse that disturbed the peace and blessings his family had enjoyed to this day.

This incident must have happened several decades after the Flood, by which time Noah's sons had their own families. It was never God's plan to have Noah curse his family. The plan leading to the curse was initiated by Satan and suited his plans to subdue the world under his own plan. This is often missed by those who are keen to limit the curse to only God and Noah. Satan wanted to use a new curse to eventually spread curses on all mankind. He wanted to resurrect the plan he had lost through the demise of Cain's generation in the flood.

Before turning to Ham's remaining three sons Cush, Mizraim and Phut, it is important to dwell on the story of Canaan. Noah died 350 years after the flood or 2006 years after man's departure from the garden of Eden. (Simple addition of individuals' ages shows this.) It is quite obvious that Canaan's family grew with the cloud of a curse over their lives and, in conformity with the nature of a curse, some inexplicable despicable behaviour and misfortune must have dogged them more than other families. The devil feeds on curses because they give him the right to interfere in people's lives. Cursed people are already accused and ready targets for hordes of demons that infest them at their will.

Psychologically, Canaan's descendants may have been subjected to inferiority complexes of their own by the rest of the family groups. This must also have affected their ability to intermarry with their cousins and it is safe to assume that Canaan's descendants may have remained a separate entity. The danger that the curse would contaminate other families must have been one of the reasons why God discouraged Nimrod's plan to unite all families under his protection at Babel and ended up confusing their tongues. The Bible story shows how God later commanded Abraham's descendants to separate themselves from the Canaanite tribes so that they would not be contaminated by the evil and demonically inspired behaviour of this cursed nation. A ruthless annihilation of many Canaanites to wipe out the curse would be given to Israelite tribes when they subdued the land of Canaan generations later.

By the time that the Babel project was abandoned, one cannot rule out the adverse impact of the influence of Canaan's family behaviour on other families. Babel has grown to be accepted as Satan's plan through Nimrod to defy God's plan for humanity to spread out over the earth. The closer they stayed together the easier the cancerous curse in Canaan's family would spread to other families. It is quite obvious that most of the labourers in the Babel project were the sons of Canaan since the curse had given the others the right to subject them to slavery. It is also reasonable to assume that many Canaanites were made personal slaves of those who scattered from Babel. A slave's incomprehension of the master's tongue has never really mattered to the master who will always get the slave to speak his tongue. Slaves in every generation have lost the pride of identity of their mother tongue.

Where was God's grace in all this? Why did He allow such injustice on Canaan? God respects boundaries. God honoured Noah and gave him authority and dominion over events for trusting and obeying Him. There are individuals in the bible who God allowed to exercise a lot of power over events and people. Individuals like Noah, Abraham, Sarah etc. seem to have been honoured so much by God that he did not openly contradict their words. If anything, God would exercise damage limitation after they had made decisions that seemed unfair or unreasonable. God would not contradict Noah and He must have reduced His cover of grace over Canaan's family in conformity with Noah's utterance. But in accordance with His role as a gracious God He was already putting in place means to rectify the damage that had been done to Ham's family.

Canaan's family was later reduced to slaves of their relatives and their labour was inherited by others. The land of their inheritance went to the Hebrew family of Shem descended from Abraham. All nations of the world from the greatest to the least have benefitted by way of the salvation story built on Canaan's labour. And the nations of the world today are locked in combat for this piece of land founded by Canaan.

God would not let Satan have his way. God turned Canaan's curse into a blessing for all mankind. What the devil meant for evil turned into inexplicable blessings. Canaan's land became known as the land of milk and honey. One of his cities, Jerusalem, became the city of the King. And God's own Son wiped Canaan's tears by becoming the cursed Son of Man, to die in the cursed land of Canaan and from this land destroy the curse of the whole world.

When God cursed the earth after Adam's fall in the Garden of Eden, it was not because God loved curses. It was because sin marries curses. After almost 2000 years during which the curse blazed its way through generations, God blessed the earth again after the Flood. As mentioned above, God's business is to bless while the devil's business is to create curses.

Over many generations man amassed so much guilt and curses as recorded in the bible by scribes and prophets. Yet God still maintained a remnant of blessing that could not be put out. In every judgement grace and mercy were also present. At the fullness of time God gave the ultimate gift to the world of His own blessed Son. The Blessing Himself came down to pay the price of the curse of the whole world. He showed that it is only the blessing that has power over the curse. In Jesus, all curses and the devil's mandate in them have been disarmed. The handwriting of ordinances that the devil held against every human being was taken out the way and nailed to the cross with Christ, including Noah's curse. (Colossians 2:14) No wonder why the three sons of Noah were represented at the cross. Ham's son(Simon of Cyrene in North Africa) carried the cross of Jesus, Japheth's son (Romans), crucified Him and Shem's son (Jews) shouted, "Crucify him!" when their paths crossed again on the cursed hill of Golgotha in the land of Canaan.

Though Christ paid the debt and became the Jubilee(year of release) of man's debt, the devil will not let his captives go free. He keeps broadcasting the curse of Noah because it is sweet music to the ears of so many people. He has raised an army of his disciples who will keep accusing Ham's children for their father's sin and through guilt, cripple their confidence to claim the blessing God has for them in Christ. They are bent on stripping naked Ham's children of all dignity and leave them on display to the world just like they believe Ham did to Noah.With these evil disciples the devil has distorted the bible story of curses and blessings. We will take a look at how the blessing denied Ham by his father, more than the curse of Canaan, may have caused the mighty power of the children of Ham to diminish so much over the years.

Chapter 5
"How are the mighty fallen!"
2 Samuel 1:19

David lamented the tragic end of Saul's dynasty with these words. The potential for greatness that was in both king Saul and David's best friend Jonathan now lay like worthless weapons on the ground. The tragic picture of the faithful and loving Jonathan, dead beside his disobedient father Saul, was such a painful reminder to David of how the errors of the parent can affect the lives of their children. King Saul had disobeyed God, who had in turn rejected him and his family. Saul invoked a curse on his family by his disobedience and by seeking counsel from the medium of Endor. Wherever God's presence and blessing cannot be sustained, even the most powerful of nations will fall.

We also learn about the importance of a blessing from Jacob's deathbed blessing of his twelve sons. He reminds his first son Reuben of his sin in sleeping with his (Jacob's) concubine. In Genesis 49:3 he sums up Reuben's future in these words, "Unstable like water thou shalt not excel." Reuben's potential was limited by this prophecy. Though his father did not curse him, the absence of a blessing in his life would limit the potential of Reuben's children for a season.

We can relate this prophecy to Ham. Though God had blessed him and his father had not directly cursed him, by denying him the father's blessing, Noah had denied him the important cutting edge that the father's blessing offers. Though Ham fulfilled his role as nation builder, his ability to sustain that momentum of greatness was limited. He lacked the wings that the father's blessing offers those who excel. God respects the role of parents to share His creative work and allocates their blessing an important role in one's life and longevity on earth. The sad demise of the glory of Hamitic nations is testimony of the fall of the mighty. The founding fathers of Hamitic nations would be shocked today how low their descendants have fallen in the world: some to a semi-primitive existence in the forests of Africa! Unless their descendants accept the blessing to excel that Jesus brings to those who had no father's blessing, they shall remain this way.

The first role model of the Cush people was Nimrod. Cush is Hebrew word for dark-skinned. Nimrod, the strongman of Babel, was an awesome figure and a pride of the Cush people. He appears to have been a religious man, with self-driven means of trying to reach God. Babel is known to have meant 'the gate of heaven'. But it was a rebellious front to God's plans for nations to spread out over the earth. He might also have preyed on the fears of another flood that might have made people to seek skyscrapers as dwellings or on their fear of wild animals roaming the environment. He became the protector of the people because of his hunting skills and some saviour-like qualities. These qualities appear to have been passed on to some African leaders. Unless God intervenes to save the people from their ambitions to build vain monuments of themselves, the future of nations is at stake. Some writers have laboured to identify Nimrod as the earliest image of antichrist but close scrutiny of scriptures appears to point at Cain more than Nimrod. This deliberate attempt to identify antichrist with Nimrod is an attempt to label black greatness with evil.

The memory of Babel has been carried away by many nations as they spread over the earth. Similar towering structures or some resemblance of it were built, for example in the Inca kingdom of Central America, Great Zimbabwe monument, pyramids of Sudan and Egypt etc.

The hunting skills of Nimrod were legendary. The young men who left Babel must have taken these skills with them to Africa where they have turned into a time-wasting and energy-consuming preoccupation of some African groups. They can be compared with the idolatrous Israelites on the wilderness journey whose aimless pleasure-loving lifestyle disgusted God. Paul warned the party-loving Corinthian church about this when he said, "Neither be ye idolaters, as were some of them: as it is written: the people sat down to eat and drink, and rose up to play." (1 Corinthians 10:7). The hunting dances, magic charms and demonic worship involved in African hunting expeditions are well known, portraying Africans as objects of primitive idolatrous entertainers. Such societies in Africa are known for their stubborn resistance to change, illiteracy, semi-primitive existence and callous destruction of animal life.

God describes the Africans in Ezekiel 30:9 as, "the careless Ethiopians..." This is strong language, coming from one's Creator. It sounds as if God was displeased by the Africans' disregard for accountability for their resources, potential and role in His plans. They seemed to have a tendency to major in minor and trivial pursuits while beasts devoured the flocks of their land. This weakness, more than other deficits, could have been the acute reason for the way Africa made herself vulnerable to exploitation by the spirit of greed that has ravaged her from within and from without. There is a joke that someone made about one of these trivial pursuits in exasperation at his African relatives' pre-occupation with polygamy. He said that when Queen Sheba travelled from the land of black people to visit King Solomon, she brought a delegation that included her senior male advisers. While she and other visitors listened to the wisdom of Solomon, her male counsellors were more interested to know how Solomon kept his hundreds of wives in line. Those, he said, were the skills they brought back to their land! God himself describes the Egyptians as unfaithful Israel's lovers "great of flesh" (Ezekiel 16:26). Some Africans' preoccupation with their generous fleshly attributes has led, in some cases, to worthless pre-occupation with sexual prowess and moral decadence which God hates in nations. This has been made worse by foreign fantasy-seekers making tourism of African flesh.

God gave Africans arguably one of the best inheritances, with good weather, almost Eden-like plant and animal life and abundant mineral and energy resources. Someone hinted that Africa failed to develop, not for want of intellectual ability, but because of overabundance of resources and inept management of them. Africa's military strength, the almost endless supply of meat and crops and predictable weather patterns made Africa almost reckless. Africa became a sitting duck to more hungry nations who were desperate for resources.

The bible story shows that God blesses people and nations who have the shepherding qualities to protect their resources and to be accountable more than those with the hunter qualities of destroying, reckless spending and unaccountability. God rejected hunters like Nimrod, Ishmael, Esau and chose shepherds like Abel, Abraham, Isaac, Jacob, Moses and David.

The bible story of the good king Hezekiah who, in 2 Kings 20, recklessly exposed the wealth of his kingdom to the Babylonian emissaries reflects Africa's case too. Just as the prophet Isaiah warned Hezekiah that this recklessness would lead to the plundering of the kingdom's treasures by these same foreigners, his prophecy could have well been made for some nice but gullible African kings and chiefs. The foreign travellers who "discovered" the African lands sent back to their countries almost unbelievable reports of a treasure mass of land waiting to be exploited. This fuelled almost unbridled greed and every immoral excuse used to exploit these resources. The rest is history: slavery followed by colonialism, neo-colonialism followed by voluntary enslavement through economic migration from Africa.

Deprivation has made Africa's children justifiably angry with those that they believe exploited them. This has led to blacks seeking to build relations with those who have their own bitter experiences of injustice of one kind or another. Black people are in danger of being exploited by every group of people with one grievance or another and ending up hating those who should be their friends. The God-built closeness between the Israelites and the blacks is being lost every day. Africans accuse Jews of looking down on them while Jews feel that Africans have chosen to take sides with those who hate them. The missed blessing of praying for the peace of Jerusalem continues to elude Africa while the friendly and respectful interaction of their patriarchs with Africa that benefitted them both has been missed by the Jews. Some blacks have welcomed every devil and his curses into their home in the name of solidarity.

The political demise of Hamitic nations

The fall of Egypt to Assyria is graphically enacted by Isaiah in Isaiah 20. Assyria takes slaves of both Egypt and Ethiopia after conquering them. Egypt at the time was ruled by an Ethiopian/Nubian monarch and Isaiah in Chapter 18 recognises this confederacy of black nations in very respectful terms like "a people terrible from their beginning" verse 2. Both Egyptians and Ethiopians are led into slavery to Assyria in semi-naked state as Isaiah prophesied in Isaiah 20. This embarrassment of the black nations who were proud and highly regarded caused God to command Isaiah to enact this sad event in figurative manner of prophecy lasting three years. The first slavery ends when Assyria's power is ended in defeat by Persian-ruled Babylon. A resurgence of both Egyptian and Ethiopian power follows the end of Assyrian slavery.

The second and more painful slavery follows during the days of prophets Jeremiah and Ezekiel. This is the 70 year Jewish exile prophesied by Jeremiah and which was years later understood and prayed into conclusion by Daniel. This slavery by Babylon put to an end the kingdom power of Israel/Judah, Assyria, Egypt and Ethiopia. Ezekiel is graphic in prophesying of messengers coming in ships to bring panic to the "careless Ethiopians". The Ethiopians appear to have over thousands of years been so self-assured of their renowned strength that they needed God to remind them of their fallibility. Babylon soon subdued both Egypt and Ethiopia and dispersed their people to the whole Persian controlled kingdom. This must have happened in the thirtieth year of Jewish exile in Babylon. The book of Esther describes this kingdom as extending from India to Ethiopia. It is at the time of Cyrus that the 70/40 year slavery ends but Assyria, Egypt or Ethiopia or indeed Israel/Judah never recover their dominance again. The end of the kingdoms of Egypt and Cushite nations are given the honour of lamentation by Ezekiel 32 because more than two thousand years of their power since Nimrod had finally come to an end. No kingdoms since then have survived so many years of dominance. Ham's descendants are indeed the mighty that have fallen and their memory described by Ezekiel 32 as of those who descend to the lowest places of hell where there is no more remembrance and where the destiny of all other present and future kingdoms of man he named shall follow.

Africa is not the only nation that God warned of judgement in the bible. Many nations have God's written judgement which have not yet been fulfilled but will surely come to pass. Therefore for Africans to conclude that they have received a raw deal from God in recent history may be premature. By the way that some nations are promoting hatred of Christ and embracing Satan, it is quite obvious that it is only a matter of God's timing before judgement falls on them. The judgement that awaits the God-forsaking world as described in Revelations will make events of the troubles of Africa just a mere newsflash on the news bulletins.

Africa was close to God's plan in the bible as we have noted. Phillip the evangelist was miraculously involved by the Spirit to hand over the gospel of God's eternal Blessing to an Ethiopian eunuch. We have predicted that follow-up missionary activity must have ensued after this. However it looks like Africa was reckless with the message of Christ and not keen to carry the cross beyond the summit of Golgotha. Together with the Jews, the African zeal in God just stalled. The baton was passed onto Japheth's children to spread the gospel and the rewards that go with it. Jesus said that the kingdom of heaven is like a hidden treasure. Those who find it have both spiritual and often material blessing for their children. The role that could have blessed Africa somehow drifted to Japheth's children.

Africa's reckless disregard for the gospel of Christ led them into the hands of deceiving spirits. The most heinous sin of ancestral and familiar demons by way of spirit mediums, witchcraft, deity and fetish priests, which is an open worship of Satan and his power is very strong in Africa and blacks outside Africa. African countries can forget about a reversal of their fortunes as individual countries as long as these demonic practices are practised and even sanctioned by their leaders. This sin is responsible for the migration of Africa's gifted children as God removes them from these heinous family sins to places where, like Abram, they can know God and become a great people. This evil is responsible for endless misfortune on nations who have dedicated themselves to devils. The hope for Africa and her children everywhere is the militant gospel that is ablaze in the land and the assault on the strongholds of such practices by new Elijah-like princes of the kingdom of God. Africa needs the serious prayers of her children inside and mainly outside the continent to break the curses that these demons spread over the land with their presence in their homes, families and communities.

In conclusion

Egypt's cruelty to the Israelites was one of Africa's enduring disgraces. After God had lifted up the name of Egypt above the nations as the breadbasket of the famine-stricken world by giving them Joseph as His personal blessing to their land, for them to turn back after Josephs' death on his relatives was cruel and unexpected. The strangling of male children, cruel labour shifts and lengthy enslavement of migrants provoked God to unprecedented judgement of the African land.

An antichrist-like Pharaoh came onto the scene in Egypt. (The birth of Israel as a nation begins with an antichrist type of dictator as does the epilogue of their nationhood under the coming antichrist.) This event so infuriates God that He warns Egypt of severe judgement if she does not free His people. The judgement that follows is compared to the judgements of Sodom and Jerusalem in Revelations 11. And in all cases two witnesses first warn of judgement before it comes. While the judgement of Sodom is by fire and brimstone, the plagues/judgements of the antichrist kingdom in Revelations 16 are very similar to those of Egypt. The bottom line is that the ghastly sin of this Israelite slavery was perpetrated by the same evil power that controlled Sodom and that will usher in the antichrist's kingdom. The judgements are an eternal testimony of God's wrath. Most of the plagues of Egypt still remain as a testimony of Africa's problems. One plague that demands our attention is the plague of the death of the first born (Exodus 11).

The plague of the death of the first born was a big blow to Africa. The first born child in the bible is related to inheritance rights and authority in the family and land. The first son was also supposed to be dedicated to God. The judgement on this God-ordained principality limited Africa's ability to give birth or to retain worthy heirs to her resources. In one way or another Satan has laid claim to this plague unchallenged over many generations and ensured that worthy heirs lose out to usurpers to the thrones. The scourge of bad leadership in Africa is the sad spectacle of many unworthy and corrupt people becoming heirs/leaders over the land of Africa. Strongmen take over where princes are not empowered. Is it any wonder that God pronounced through the Psalmist that Princes shall come out of Africa (Psalm 68). Yes, God restored the first son to Africa: princes for every role should rise out of Africa! The Firstborn of all things, Jesus needed to live in Africa as a promise that God would not forget to resurrect the first born of Africa. Those who know the Lord will have to challenge Satan's claim in Africa, plunder his house and call forth those worthy princes with their prayers. For without their prayers "the children are come to the birth, and there is not strength to bring forth."(Isaiah 37:3)

In the meantime it is important for Africa to examine herself and be honest about the causes of some of the problems that befall her. A lengthy reflection into curses that bedevil Africa follows. It is hoped that a reader wanting to make sense of the problems in his life and that of his community may learn something from the following Chapter, repent and seek deliverance from Christ.

Chapter 6
The mystery of Africa's curses

Background

A curse is like a door that sin opens to the enemy into the life of an individual or that of a community. The curse gives the devil and his demons almost unrestricted right into that entity to disease, violate character, impoverish and destroy. When Adam sinned by disobeying God's command in the Garden of Eden, God merely decreed the curse that sin had earned each of them. Adam's curse gave Satan a claim in his family, and the enemy used Cain to kill his younger brother. To a large extent, God reduced the impact of Cain's cursed children on the post- flood generations by ensuring that not one of Cain's descendants survived the flood. Only their inventive skills were passed on to survivors of the flood. God has always intervened to rid the world of a curse. It is important to recognise that none of Cain's descendants are found in the land of Ham or anywhere in the world today. Some mischievous theologians have suggested that Cain's mark was the dark skin of black people.

When Ham sinned by seeing his father's nakedness, Canaan's family received his curse. As we observed above, God turned the curse into a blessing for the whole world. This must have frustrated Satan immensely. However, God also ensured that those Canaanite groups most affected by the curse were either judged by fire eg Sodom or later annihilated by the Israelites when they possessed their inheritance. God was even prepared to save the cities of Sodom and Gomorrah if only five righteous persons had been found in them. But it is quite clear that He showed mercy to many Canaanites and even honoured them. Some even were chosen as Christ's disciples. In wrath God has always shown mercy (Habakkuk 3).We have also noted above that the popular so-called curse of Ham does not stand the scrutiny of scripture. Satan has been the one using people to establish a stronghold of a curse mentality on Ham's descendants.

An example of how desperate Satan is for a curse befalling a nation is when he stirred up Balaam the sorcerer to lay a curse on Israel (Numbers 23). With all her blessings, Israel needed God's timely intervention to avert this curse. By His grace God covered whatever sin the blundering Israelite nation may have harboured and Balaam declared that he had seen no evil in Israel. He ended up blessing Israel instead. However, the devil still waited for the Israelites to be enticed into sexual sin by Balak's people so that he could invoke judgement upon them. Satan has been an accuser from the beginning. He also remains an accuser of the children of Ham to this day.

There are many descendants of Noah who have never forgiven Ham for seeing their father naked. They stand with Satan before God accusing Ham's children forever before God. They are quite eager to forgive others for nailing Christ on the cross more than they are to forget this sin. Even the nations that have killed millions of Jewish and Ham's children are not accorded the same severity of judgement by their fellow humans as the children of Ham.

Christians in Africa struggle to balance their understanding of curses. Many have repeatedly been reminded that they are the descendants of "cursed" Ham and have believed it. They have been told that because of the curse, Ham's descendants became dark-skinned and were driven away into the forests of Africa where they lived like savages before foreigners thankfully 'discovered and civilized them'. Many Africans deny the role of foreigners civilising them since they insist that they were already civilised and settled by the time foreigners arrived on their land. What they do not deny though is that the advent of foreigners in Africa was God's time for a rapid change towards industrialisation moving into Africa. Ten Japhethic nations from Europe, including the new America, were actively involved in the distributing of Ham's children, land and resources culminating in the historical partition of Africa in 1884. The season of explosion in knowledge prophesied by Daniel had come to pass. And in often cruel ways Africa's easy life was shaken violently. Africa would never be the same again.

This was like the birth pangs of a new Africa. Africa was caught up in a new distribution of nations with new settlements in Australia, Americas and remote places. Like Daniel had prophesied, men were now running to and fro and settling all over the world(Daniel 12:4). Japheth's blessings to be enlarged was coming into being. (Remember that God did not destroy blessings but came to destroy curses.) He was being entrusted with enlarging man's knowledge to a level God wanted. God's kingdom is a very sophisticated kingdom. The bits and pieces of knowledge that He has shared with humanity recently is just a fraction of His advanced kingdom. The glory of human inventions will look like childish toys when God reveals His own glory. And God's kingdom will only be revealed when man's kingdoms have attained and exhausted their perfection of beauty.

Kingdom building is always a painful experience. The birth of the end-time kingdoms of man which began with the resurgence of European nations was painful, established on the blood and labour of humanity. Two world wars were also fought in the process. Like the kingdom of Solomon which signified the apex of Israel's power and beauty which was built on the bloodshed in David's hands and the labour of the children of Israel, man's kingdoms have always been built on blood and human labour. In pitiful ways and with far-reaching damage Africa's children were torn from their motherland and forever separated from the root of their family tree. Many of them, just like those who remained on African soil have lived in perplexity of the evil done to their motherland and the often prevailing wind of misfortune that blows in Africa and seems to dog her children in foreign lands. As an African in a foreign land I have taken time to reflect on some lifestyles that I strongly believe attract curses in our motherland. I do not find this a condemnation of my motherland but a sober reflection of what lifestyles contradict the biblical standards and could hinder our motherland from rising again and reclaiming her position in His eyes.

Examples of curses related to Africa

Several encounters between Africans and Hebrews in the bible describe embarrassing lust for sexual gratification. Pharaoh's lust for Abraham's wife and Potiphar's wife's lust for Joseph (Genesis 39) summed the account. Some communities in Africa have for centuries practiced unmarried sex freely subjecting themselves to God's curses on immoral nations and recently to the scourge of deadly sexually transmitted diseases. Lewd and amorous sexually suggestive dances export themselves with a black person's label all over the world.

There are countries in Africa whose sexually suggestive dances are sources of national revenue. Some foreign countries are exporting their fantasies and evil lifestyles to Africa and a form of tourism to engage in sexual fantasies with Africans promotes cursed immoral lifestyles. Some churches describe exorcising individuals possessed by sexual demons that use human bodies to gratify their insatiable desire for sex, while some describe sexual demons that possess individuals and sexually seduce people in their sleep. Love charms and portions are also said to be seriously used to seduce individuals for sexual advantage. There are reports of some Christians seeking deliverance from these kinds of demonic forces in churches in Africa. Sexual perversion remains a tool that the devil is using to keep Africa beset with a strong curse.

The spirit of Jacob's sons that sold Joseph to the Ishmaelites has found a home in Africa. After selling many of their brothers and sisters to slavery over the years, some Africans still continue in human trafficking and enslavement of their fellowmen. While some nationalities will defend one another, black people will most usually take sides against their own. This is also no different with black people in the diaspora who may not defend their own black colleagues even at work places. This, together with the spirit of Judas which betrayed his Master, means faithful friends and relatives are getting rare in Africa. They curse one another by speaking evil of one another. Africa and her children need to learn to love one another like Jesus taught.

Africa is also beset by some religions that promote hatred and murder of those outside their faiths. While they pretend to offer a form of godliness, they fail to teach the concept of love and peace that Africa desperately needs. Only the Prince of Peace, Jesus, can bring peace to Africa. Any black person who finds himself in a religion that promotes hatred of fellowmen who do not worship like them should know they have not found the true God.

While most of the world is learning to respect human life, taking human life remains a simple thing in Africa. It is as if Africa itself and the world are growing desensitised with the blood of black people and not placing the same value they attach to other nationalities' blood. It has become easier to forgive murderers for spilling African blood than that of other nationalities. The blood of many victims like Abel cries for vengeance everyday in Africa. While other nations will go to the end of the world to rescue one of their nationalities, African leaders will rarely lift a finger for one of their own. The blood of the innocents is shed by leaders and relatives alike, bringing curses on the land. African leaders need to hear the word of God and lead their nations in the fear and love of God.

Africa is cursed with a leadership that does not love the people they lead. While other leaders of the world are happy when their subjects succeed and prosper, African leaders feel threatened by the success of their subjects. Those in leadership seek a spectator society from the perpetual audience of the poor in the land who will stare in amazement at their prosperity. Their policies are made to curse their subjects with poverty. They care less about the poverty of their people. Politics itself has often become a curse of Africa, with endless disregard for fairness, vote- rigging, violence, power buying, rival eliminations and tribalism. Foreign nations also use the same fragile political machinery, often to complicate the process by sometimes misinformed and self-serving interests and conveniently blame it on the abundant and willing hordes of restless unemployed and misguided young people.

The scourge of ruthless young men ready to kill for a living and for some semblance of power is common in Africa. Many angry and desperate young men and women laden by misfortunes in their lives that they cannot understand or are unable to get rid of, lose any sense of values and wish no one else any good in their lives. They become the breeding grounds of rebel groups and armed gangs churning out more curses on themselves and the communities through bloodshed of the innocent. They become the hives of demons that roam the land feeding on and fuelling curses. The devil in the serpent was cursed to forever feed on the dust of the cursed earth. Since then the devil has slid on the ground of the whole world looking for curses to feed on. That's the only sacrifice God allowed him to receive from the earth. The devil will not leave a community where curses are readily available. In communities where vision is lacking, people perish. Christ is desperately needed to restore the vision of Africa's children.

One way to restore vision to Africa is through education. The scourge of illiteracy in African communities is the reason why the enemy has many willing, easily manipulated young adults to engage in prostitution, robbery, promotion of accursed traditional practices and all forms of vice. Many African leaders prefer an uneducated population which is incapable of challenging them and can be satisfied with so little while eking out an existence in the remote places of the country. To think that it was Africa that invented the 365 day calendar in Egypt speaks volumes of how capable Africans are with the right education. The missionaries to Africa will forever be remembered for prioritising education together with spiritual awareness. Without good education Africa will remain the tourist destination of foreign entertainment houses seeking semi-primitive lifestyles.

Closely linked with this scourge is the curse of theft that is very common among those who have no fear of God in them. Organised theft of the nation's infrastructure itself is often alarming, with massive plundering of equipment, medicine, aid for the poor, cables that are meant to supply electricity, water and communication. This almost senseless plunder is demonic in nature, meant to frustrate the development of the nation. This is related to the plague of Egyptian locusts that Moses prayed God to be rid of the land. A massive wind had to wrestle this scourge into the Red sea (Exodus 10:18-19). This bore a resemblance to the legions of demons of Gadara that had to be cast out of their human base on land into the sea. Where Christ is not Master, the devil, who is the master thief comes to teach our children to steal and destroy.

Another more subtle curse of Africa is the curse of aid in itself. I have lived in communities where aid was given to undeserving individuals who sold it for personal gains. The culture of expecting aid has encouraged laziness among some communities while absolving politicians of responsibility to their own electorate. While the concept of aid is noble in itself, the source of the aid may sometimes be a curse for African recipients. Aid collected from old women posing naked for such funds is definitely cursed source. Hoping to bless Africa with cursed money is not a blessing. Western societies would not accept similar sources of aid coming from Africa because they have a sense of personal pride. What Africa needs more is blessings that will rid them of the curse of perpetual aid.

Ties that bind

While strong family ties should be a blessing, unfortunately in Africa it has become a source of shared curses. The traditional African family is bound together by bonds of clanship immersed in spiritual maze with some rumoured to be based on human sacrifice. African families have perfected the art of demonic worship into a subtle form of entertainment. Families are brought together, from the bank executive to the cattle herder, and led by the clan elders, bathe in magic portions, with chanting and animal sacrifices to demons. Whole families become addicted to this form of worship, edged on with riotous feasting and drunkenness. Everyone carries away the curse with them wherever they go. The devil 'blesses' some of them because they have bowed the knee to him. They mistake this success to a blessing from God and are effectively deceived by the devil. There are many families in Africa whose wealth has come from the devil. It does not come with peace but with more demands for spirit worship and endless family feuds. Partaking of such wealth of the wicked is extremely damaging on Christians! God has had to literally command some individuals to come out of the Ur of their fathers to other lands before He can deliver them from the tentacles of these strong family ties.

Jealousy and envy remain a strong curse of Africa. Clans are torn apart by jealousy and individuals seek the charms of witches to invoke misfortune on the successful in the community. Families are laden with the graves of promising young people who were mysteriously killed by jealousy relatives. It is often the curse of deprived people that they will not bear to welcome change for the better for one of their own. They would prefer an outsider getting a blessing than one of their own. While other nations would open doors and ideas that enrich their fellowmen, many black people tend to keep enriching secrets from fellow blacks. They often rightly complain that enriching a fellow black can create sudden competition and ungrateful response after they have made it. Dishonourable and self-destroying behaviour inherited from ancestors needs a trip to the Manufacturer Himself who alone can make new people out of people of chronically unreliable nature.

Black communities often complain about a crisis of expectations that exists with those close to them. How often do black people despair about friends and close ones who they show love and dedication to who treat them in return despitefully and deceitfully. It is often reported how some black people tend to respect, like and even adore those who treat them as nothing. It is often the sad result of many years of subjection to abusive relationships that individuals grow confused with their loyalties and fall victim to the curse of Delilah(Judges 16). The curse of Delilah dominates a lot of relationships; full of flattery, scheming and bleeding of divine anointing. Many Samsons, full of devotion and blind trust in the goodness of those they adore often lose their spiritual vision after getting betrayed by other blacks including black Christians.

The devil has succeeded in dividing the tribes of Africa into clans dedicated to demonic deities. Strangers are fiercely segregated from these communities and blamed for misfortune on the communities. Often tribal disputes arise leading to bloodshed and endless chains of warfare. Often a form of Christian faith without evidence of the new birth masks the face of these conflicts. Africa is cursed with the leadership of a lot of clergy that is not born again and that practices traditional demonic works in secret or a strong charismatic prophesying demonic front that pretends to be practising the true works of Christ.

Of particular concern are social lifestyles that attract curses in Africa. God is clear about his heart for widows and children. Unfortunately many traditionally-based communities in Africa have cruel and heinous attitudes to widows whom they often falsely blame for the deaths of their husbands, dispossessing them of all rights to property and subjecting them and their helpless children to abject poverty and homelessness. Such communities attract the curse of the tears of the widows and children and this curse in turn is passed to their own families. There are specific angels in charge of widows and children who appear often on their behalf before the face of God. Christians sometimes try to explain this kind of curse inherited from such offending parents as generational curses. Another generational curse common in Africa is the abuse of disabled people. Name-calling, open abuse, neglect and segregation of disabled and mentally unwell people is common in many communities attracting curses that are passed on to children. Closely related with it is the pride of those who make it in black communities. Looking down on those who struggle and mocking them is very common even among believers. Whole nations have been cursed with misfortune and economic problems because of this pride.

Parental abuse also bedevils families in Africa. Misrepresentation of Christian faith is often used to deny parents their due respect which is heretically passed on to 'new spiritual parents' in the faith. This missed balance of doctrine produces believers who hate their parents and curse their roots, being led to associate everything evil with their parents. Not only are they in danger of having their days shortened in this life for disrespect of their parents but they are in danger of boasting themselves of tomorrow when they do not know what a day may bring (Proverbs 27:1). Some successful children no longer want to be associated with their lowly parentage and neglect their parents, bringing shame to themselves and their community. If these children cared to develop their lowly communities, then they would see rapid change in the status of their land. Parental abuse under any guise attracts significant curses.

Idleness or laziness is another curse in Africa. As someone born and bred in Africa I have painful and disheartening experiences of families whose poverty is merely a result of the idleness of the sluggard of Proverbs 6:6-11 who knows no better than ants. I have known families which are usually the target of the media looking for sad pictures and stories, ready to come to cameras to embarrass themselves and their community. They are best at blaming everyone else except themselves for their poverty. But when the rains fall they don't go to their fields to plant anything. They prioritise pleasures like hunting, dancing, drinking and endless talk to catering for their children. No amount of aid seems to resolve their poverty. Even in a land where poles, water, grass and clay are free, they cannot be bothered to construct a neat house. It has been proven that when churches in Africa start teaching believers about working hard, saving their money and being thrifty, significant changes have been observed in the changes of their living circumstances. God works with careful and thrifty individuals not with careless and reckless individuals.

Closely linked with idleness is the curse of self-neglect. God makes it clear that He wants cleanliness. He strongly advised Moses to instruct the Israelites to wash themselves and their clothes before coming before Him at the mount of Sinai (Exodus 19:10).Unwashed individuals and strong dirty body odours are repugnant to God. Growing up in Africa, I have often wondered how a fisherman who spends the day at the river went about unwashed. Worship of demons and devils have drawn some African groups towards filthy costumes, body paints and markings that make them look like the devils they worship.

Snuff-snorting, dirty unclean teeth and general poor hygiene have often made some of our people look wretched. There has been amazing changes observed once they became Christians. The word of God brings a new awareness in self-care. Cleanliness is often evidence of a blessing.

Making and issuing curses

Many have grown up in societies where curses are very commonly made and respected. Some families in Africa have the backing of familiar avenging spirits that fulfil their curses. It is common practice for parents and relatives to curse children in anger. Some children only escape these curses when they get desperate about misfortunes in their lives and seek church leaders to help them. When, by the grace of God, they meet anointed men of God, the yoke of curses is broken and changes begin in their lives. Yet with this new freedom they still remain frightened of curses. The devil uses fear to get them to recreate new mental chains that rebuild strongholds over their lives. And this fear is often channelled through dreams, experiences, well-founded superstitions and misrepresentation of the word of God.

They also believe in cursing their enemies. They are easily misled by the devil when they become Christians and still feel they can use curses on their enemies in the name of Jesus. These kinds of witchcraft prayers are not answered by God. They are hijacked by Satan who gladly gains access into their fellow believers' lives who are not strong in the word and knowledge of God. People who believe that they are cursed have a curse stronghold over their lives and need to be delivered to grasp the concept of blessing. It is often pitiful how some African pastors have taken advantage of their fearful Christian flock to keep them in bondage to the fear of endless curses related to dreams, ancestry and normal human failures. An endless line of deliverance ministers has hijacked the important role of deliverance in the African church and by exaggerating its need have made lucrative careers out of it. Only reintroducing the teaching of the power of the cross will give these traumatised believers relief from their fears.

Some Christians have been known to keep holding onto some practice of their ancestral deities which they have trusted for years. It is not very easy to believe in faith for solution to some things that traditional process could offer quicker or easier: especially when one has been hurt by a person who will not be bothered to apologise. In the past a visit to a medicine man would procure a magic portion that could be directed as a curse at the offender. The joy of quick revenge usually followed and the offender often learnt his lesson well and left you alone. This is contradicted by the Christian teaching to pray for your enemies and leaving God to avenge in His own time. Impatient Christians find themselves tempted to use the bible to curse their enemies. Or they may find themselves misled into some religious pseudo-pentecostal groups who mix the bible and traditional power to satisfy this quest for revenge or justice or their obsession with prophecies.

Africans who get born again need to ask God to give them the spirit of love, of mercy and of seeking the promotion of their neighbours. The secret of other nations' success is the willingness of their people to help their neighbours to make it like them. And the secret of those who are given this help is to show gratitude and not to dishonestly defraud the hand that is helping them. But the sad experiences of relatives and friends who abuse the help given them has led to a hardening of attitudes of the benevolent individuals in African communities. As generous individuals withdraw their hands, some more deserving cases are cursed with perpetual poverty.

Having grown up in hate-filled envious and deprived communities, it is often difficult to understand love, often mistaking show-offish pride-driven giving for a loving spirit. It is therefore important to be prayerful in identifying subjects of our giving so that we do not "throw pearls to swine" who will turn to attack us.

Real evil power

Africa has a peculiar sin that keeps curses multiplying on its land. This problem has its roots in the earliest record of the land of Ham in the bible. It is the ability to work demonic wonders and deadly witchcraft. This was witnessed when Pharaoh's magicians stood before Pharaoh and Moses. They were able to compete with God's power in three significant signs and wonders. They also turned their rods into serpents showing that they had power to invoke significant demonic power that Christ specifically told His disciples He would empower them to crush. He promised them power to tread on serpents and scorpions and over all the power of the enemy. The magicians also turned water into blood, showing significant powers over nature itself and to invoke powers of bloodshed on the land. They then imitated the plague of frogs which are closely related to lying and miracle-working spirits which proceed from the mouth of the devil, the false prophet and the beast (Revelations 16:13). Though they got stuck with the rest of the plagues, God had allowed us access into the immense treasure of power that these African magicians had. Egypt was the Babylon of knowledge and mysteries in Africa at that time. Human behaviour would suggest that these magicians were chief instructors of these dark arts to budding magicians. The art of some very dark secrets of witchcraft are treasured in Africa.

Those who have lived in Africa and are honest enough to admit the mysterious forces that rule communities there will tell of powers that make the Harry Potter magical tricks look like childish play. The explosion of Pentecostal churches in Africa is partly spurred by communities who are tired of the vengeful power of witchcraft on their lives and are seeking true power that can swallow these serpentine activities. We are not talking about silly magical pranks that magicians edit on TV. The magic that is found in Africa is vicious, murderous and gruesome and often driven by envy, jealousy and greed of every kind. Families often describe sad accounts of sudden and mysterious deaths of whole families. While the western world is spending millions to clone living beings, the existence of strange animal and human life is well narrated in African communities. The art of invisibility is also well developed in some African communities. The kind of experiences that Pentecostal believers encounter as they exorcise individuals who are either possessed, stricken or who practice the witchcraft arts would sound comical to uninitiated ears. Civilised and educated foreign pastors who venture into Africa have often been called to dig deep into God's power when they encountered some of these forces. Africa is the testing ground of those who claim to have the power of God.

Satan has set off a chain effect on African communities besieged by these forces. Those who don't know Christ seek the power of medicine men who in turn use demonic power to protect them. From the frying pan into the fire, the people are held in the grasp of fear by community oracles, shrines and satanic priests who intervene to make sense of their plight. The deceitful manner by which individuals are driven to consult familiar spirits of their gods who in turn punish the evildoer is a clear example of froglike, filthy activities climbing over windows, doors and walls of homes. Those who do not know the depth of Satan as they should, think that the devil is always a liar. The devil's art is his deceit. He can tell the truth as long as it will lead to deceit in the end. Familiar spirits are capable of prophesying the truth, unravelling mysteries with correct answers and reading people's minds. If they lied most of the time, communities would not hold them in such high regard. When one considers how individuals can fly from a foreign land to consult a shrine in an obscure African village and go back satisfied, can underline how powerful and well organised this deceit is.

The curse of fear

A nagging persistence of adversity seems to bedevil fearful people. The propensity for something going horribly wrong is greater in fearful communities. Because they expect something to go wrong, it will often do. The devil and his demons can smell fear the way dogs do. When Christ becomes Lord, the Spirit of God inside us is greater than the fears in the world.

Superstition has remained an enduring curse of Africa and her children. Based on signs and wonders of demons, the origins of these superstitions are not baseless. Children growing up in communities where elders talk of fearful repercussions to everyday events are bound to grow up frightened of the unknown. Where Christ has not been welcome, the lines have been drawn by the devil. These superstitions have been the cause for tribal warfare and stubborn resistance to change.

Even some born again Africans still struggle with superstitions and find themselves at odds with the Christian law of liberty and God's faithfulness. By keeping a constant lookout for a devil who is out to get them through friends and enemies alike, it is often sad to find superstitious believers binding and rejecting imaginary evil everywhere. It is the word we speak in faith that matters instead of the word we speak in fear. It is also easy to lose faith in a faithful God who takes care of us and our loved ones and who protects us when we sleep. We do not take care of ourselves. God does. No amount of binding and rejecting can cover our souls. The ever-present cover of the blood and fire of the Holy Ghost destroys every dart of thoughts, words or curses that are said against us. The angel of the Lord is assigned to protect us. We need to learn again to be trusting like children, and asking God in prayer to take care of us so that we can relax in God's mighty hands.

As stated above, it is important to repeat that some African pastors have unfortunately built their ministries and careers on these fears of their superstitious brothers, threatening to make their liberty in Christ of very little effect. Exaggerated spiritual stress on curses, dreams and normal poor human judgement in everyday business has become a new threat to true deliverance. They have removed the integral teaching of the power of the cross in the life of the believer and his family which ensures deliverance in our day to day testimony.

The scourge of terror of the supernatural has bedevilled Africa over many generations. African communities seem to be cursed with demons of fear that have infiltrated their families and impacted very negatively on their rationalisation of reality. Night has become the time of terrifying occurrences in some African societies, when evil power seems unleashed on homes. A pattern of explaining things unknown or misunderstood in supernatural ways has developed over many generations to the extent of inhibiting change, discovery and normal human curiosity. Demonic signs and wonders have been played on African minds for many centuries and passed on to their descendants without questions. The advent of western education has in recent centuries given rise to questioning of some of these strongly-held fears though with very limited success. Some educated individuals have simply put an educated mask over their inherited beliefs but never really been delivered from them. Only the advent of the gospel with Holy Ghost power has infiltrated the strongholds that bind both the educated and uneducated Africans and set them at liberty. Today, Africa has a growing generation of people who can openly challenge mental strongholds that the devil has created over many centuries.

The curse of enduring mystery of the prosperous evil

The almost inexplicable mystery of evil, big brother-like individuals who prosper, live long and are almost untouchable by life's problems has baffled people throughout every generation. Those who have no fear or care for God somehow tend to have it their way to the extent of frustrating those who fear God, who may never know a fraction of their ease of life. This is acutely felt in many deprived societies and particularly in Africa where their oppressors, exploiters and abusers who are both foreign and indigenous have the tyrannical Cain-like God-forsaking character but prosper, live long and leave wealth to their children. Even those Christians who expect a lottery kind of blessing in their lives by using God's faith gospel, find themselves unable to compete with these individuals.

A sad picture of the church is emerging in Africa today. It is the image of Christians whose hands have been soiled by the prosperity of these prosperous wicked. Just as the Cain generation so overwhelmed the righteous generation of Seth before the Flood, so is the prosperous evil in government and positions of power in Africa soiling the hands of covetous believers. A new parallel of evil living at peace side by side with the church is emerging. We now have Christian leaders who have lost their cutting edge over demons that they fail to exorcise them from those who flee for deliverance into the church. This strategy of the devil is being used effectively against the church in corrupt societies. The devil is using the prosperous evil to soil the hands of the deprived but fervent believers. They exchange their cutting edge for the deals that enrich them. The hope for the prosperity-mad church in the world is the simple unadulterated faith and power that should define Africa's church. Can Africa be entrusted custody of the future of God's truth and power? If this vision is to be realised then repentance must again start in the house of God. Only a repentant church with clean hands can break the curse of corruption in African nations. Otherwise evil will increase while we boast of revival every day.

Some preachers in Africa have imported means to comfort restless Christians by promising them a coming transfer of the wealth of the wicked. With all due respect to those few who feel they have benefitted this way, it is often misleading to emphasise this to the church because the model of Christ's blessing is different from that of the wicked. First, Christ's blessing brings the priceless blessing of eternal assurance of unimaginable wealth in New Jerusalem. Secondly this blessing gives us comfort, health and joy in this life. It often comes with material wealth to those gifted to be 'helps' to the body of Christ. Lastly the blessing also comes with the blessing, not curse, of trials and tribulations. Trials and tribulations can easily be confused with curses by the dogmatic doctrines of some zealous pastors. Equating this blessing to the almost undisturbed prosperity of the prosperous evil is to raise unreal and unbiblical expectations on believers. The curse of the sin of covetousness has now moved into some churches in Africa where people should be free.

Modern believers are poorly equipped to discern the difference between curses and the blessing of trials with tribulations, persecution and the virtue of patience in endurance. By being spoon-fed a gospel that uses the wealth of the wicked as the model to emulate, they have been misled into thinking that the persecuted disciples and those who endured untold trials were cursed and would have needed deliverance! Can modern believers comprehend their superstar-like pastors getting beaten and brutalised and even killed like other believers over past generations? Are they able to comprehend that the grace of rights that protects us from persecution doesn't make those who suffer persecution less able to claim God's promises on protection?

Believers need to be equipped to understand that God's promises of perfect health, perfect peace and security and debt-free wealth are the standards of the Kingdom blessings we are assured as we seek first the kingdom of heaven and His righteousness and not just a name-it and have-it biblical supermarket. Just as the promise of eternal life demands our denying of our lives unto death, these similar promises come with dying to self and dying to covetousness. The children of the Kingdom in Africa will never overcome the Cain-like lifestyles of the world by living like them. God is preparing a virgin from Africa who will be custodian of His Truth which a Babylonian lifestyle in some foreign churches are prostituting.

Another righteous man, Job, also despaired about these prosperous wicked individuals in Job 12:6 when he complained that, "The tabernacle of robbers prosper, and they that provoke God are secure; into whose hand God bringeth abundantly." David recognised this controversy in his Psalm 37:1 when he advised those with similar perplexity saying, "Fret not thyself because of evildoers, neither be thou envious against the workers of iniquity." Righteous individuals in the Kingdom of God need to know that God will bless them at His own pace and that they should be grateful of the level of blessings He bestows on them at every level. Competing with the Cain personalities in Africa and abroad by using God's word is missing our calling. Poor believers are often victims of this get-rich quick lottery gospel because in their desperation to escape their poverty they are ready to take high risk.

It is obvious that since the first offender Cain, who God branded with a mark of longevity and protection from avengers, a line of similarly branded persons seems to continue in this world. Satan has a claim of such individuals in families in every generation. We should be grateful for Jesus that the new covenant in Christ gives us access to God to pray for our families so that the model of our families is not built on the old covenant where the devil's claim in families was almost assured of a Cain seed. Africa surely needs to be rid of this seed. (For further reading please proceed to Notes Chapter 3 on the 'Cain project'.)

Disarming curses with blessings

Christ has disarmed the power of curses for those who know His word. He has given us the power to diffuse the power of curses by which demons have land-mined our communities. He has also commanded his disciples to bless and not curse: because those who curse stand by Satan's side in the court of heaven as accusers of their brethren. Africa and her children are desperately in need of people who bless others because they are already burdened by people who have inherited the venom of the serpent to curse with their tongues. Angry and unhappy individuals who are not at peace with themselves are known to swear and curse more than happy people. As Christ sets us free from the bitterness of our souls, we should learn the new language of blessing and discard the swearing and cursing of our fathers and mothers which has kept our land besieged with the venomous spirit of ill-will. The wind of ill-will which blows all the time among Africa and her children are often pedalled by her own people.

Those who know the Lord should also understand that curses will not merely leave their lives because someone is praying for them or because they are giving to the church. It is poor knowledge of God to believe that witches or relatives are cursing us when we are cursing ourselves with our sinful lives. We have a sad generation of believers who do not know to take responsibility for their faults or sins and will blame everyone else and imagined enemies for things not going well in their lives. They also believe that seeking forgiveness from God on a regular basis is a sign of little faith. Blessings and sin are opposites. Christians who have poor characters keep curses in their families and the flow of blessings is blocked by these sins. They should learn to be humble again and follow Christ's example who taught us to pray, "Forgive us our trespasses" because while we are on earth we should constantly search our hearts and allow His light to expose that which is uncharacteristic of God's new nature in us.

God is grooming a bride from His black people who will bear blessings and not curses to their communities and the whole world. He wants to use His born-again children to open channels/rivers of blessings to their communities. As He used the children of Israel to bring blessings to nations, He is using the children of the Kingdom to do the same. Africa stands more in need of a blessing than aid. And the bride is the well of that blessing and Christ has healed the bitter waters of her troubled life. The blessing is the key that Africa and her children need to unlock the rivers of milk and honey of her many resources. The blessing will give her wisdom, peace and goodwill and lift her people up from the dust of despair. Intercessors should always ask the Lord to rain blessings on Africa. Blessings will diffuse the poisonous dust of the curse that clings to our land. Let our voices call on the Lord to rain blessings on our land. He will do so. Let Africa's children start declaring the eternal blessing of Israel to each other in the name of Jesus:

> The Lord bless thee, and keep thee:
> The Lord make His face shine upon thee, and be gracious unto thee:
> The Lord lift up His countenance upon thee, and give thee peace."(Numbers 6:24-26)

African Christians should grasp the fact that we are vehicles of the Lord's blessing. Our joy is complete when we bless. Christians who curse others will never know peace in their own lives because they are disobedient to Christ who instructed us to bless and not to curse. Jealousy disciples of Christ who try to curse the ministries of others slow down their own progress. If they truly believe that one African minister is using the devil's power in their ministry, why don't they come together with others and bind the strongman's power behind that ministry and plunder his kingdom? Cursing other Christians is similar to digging a pit that God will let you fall in yourself. (See NOTES for further reading where we trace the age-old source of curses and see why Christians should have no part in promoting curses in this world.)

Chapter 7
The great lie: Satan's great delusion

2 Thessalonians 2:11: "And for this cause God shall send them strong delusion, that they should believe a lie."

God chose the timeframe for the writing of the bible. By choosing mainly Jewish writers to write the Bible was out of His wisdom. The bible seems very silent on race issues and dwells more on how nations, irrespective of who they are, are blessed or judged for their works and not for their colour. As we have seen, the bible story's footsteps are found in the lands of the cursed Canaan, and other descendants of Ham with very little involvement of Japheth's sons who feature towards the end of the Bible story as Greeks and Romans. Not only does Africa struggle with curses, she also has to struggle with an assault on her people by a devil-inspired and devil-deluded machinery of lies and prejudice.

The devil has been furious with the way the bible was written. Besides trying over the years to destroy the bible and both the sons of Ham and Shem who were mainly used by God in shaping the bible story, he has also tried to rewrite the bible.

Jesus said that the devil was a liar and murderer from the beginning. True enough, the first two characteristics of Satan we know about are his lie in Eden and his murderous inspiration of

Cain. With these two tools he has terrorised the children of Ham and Shem. There are no two nations that have suffered from lies and bloodshed more than the children of Ham and Shem. Whoever hates them has a powerful and enduring reason for it. Maybe their destinies are entwined as was their past.

Millions of Ham's children have been killed through slave trade and callous murder and continue to die every day from wars sponsored by others. The same has happened to Shem's children, mainly of Jewish group and recently of various other Shemite groups. They have also been scattered throughout the world and millions have been murdered over the ages and in genocides and holocaust. They also continue to be murdered today by wars sponsored by others. Both these families are hated and despised all over the world with a passion. On top of that, the most vicious tool that has been waged against them has been by the lie of the devil.

The devil has gone out with a vicious machinery to lie against the bible story, try to change its actors' nationalities, and add new texts to the bible. Every day we have reports of some archaeological discovery to change the bible story or the discovery of some lost book of the bible to change the bible story. The aim of the devil is to destroy the authenticity of the bible as we know it and bring in other actors of his choice. Now we have gospels of Judas Iscariot, the Grail etc surfacing from the devil's pit. The devil's disciples have written these texts and falsely dated them to challenge the bible story. These types of lies will increase and Christians who flirt with them will have their faith shaken badly and their potentials never realised. 2Peter1:16 refers to these kind of lies when he says, "For we have not followed cunningly devised fables, when we made known unto you the power and coming of our Lord Jesus Christ.." These lies, which are well crafted fables by demonically inspired secret groups will catch many deceived people in their nets and take them to hell.

The next tool is the tool of Hollywood. Holly is a tree used in magic charms by witches. The deception of editing and drama has charmed the world to believe things that are not true. Hollywood has been used by the devil's agents to produce movies that portray some bible stories in the most pathetic of ways. Some of the most intelligent bible characters like Noah, Abraham and Moses are portrayed as some confused demented personalities. Most actors in the movies are cast as non-dark - skinned to distort the role of other nations. Egypt has been the focus of some of these deceitful movies because the devil will not allow dark- skinned people credit for the role that part of Africa played in the bible.

Archaeology is another tool that the devil has hijacked to distort the bible. The immense interest in Egypt's mummies is in some cases driven by some radically racist Egyptologists who hope to disprove the role of dark-skinned Pharaohs or the Jewish slavery. Though recent excavations of dark-skinned mummies have grossly embarrassed these archaeologists, very little corrective publicity is given such issues and the smear campaign continues. The archaeological findings all over Africa of highly developed founder kingdoms have been downplayed to the laughable extent of claims that the Zulu king Tshaka's brilliance as a commander was learnt from a foreign general or that the Great Zimbabwe ruins were built by non-black people.

Japhetic writers, artists, sculptors have had almost two thousand years to make images of the bible characters that they wanted and that fitted their interpretation. That has contributed to black people getting offended by the foreign image of all bible characters which does not resemble them. Is it any wonder why God forbade the making of images resembling heavenly things in His law?

The media is another tool that has been hijacked and focussed on Africa's failed cases with so little coverage on any success. The sorry picture of rickety pole and dagga dwellings often receives more coverage of Africa while the beautiful homes nearby are ignored, because they do not convey the required media message. Some writers tried to disinherit Africans to the extent of denying that they were Ham's children but descendants of some evolved savage species. Portraying Africans as incapable of intelligent inventions or organised planning, has been used to erase the role of Ham's children from the bible and modern achievements

The other lie is to portray Canaanite tribes as Shemites. This is obviously untrue because the bible which is the true record names the Canaanite tribes and their parent names as descendants of Ham. The Canaanites are also not the children of Cush and using Canaan's curse to point at Africa's problems is not accurate. The same media portrays Jews as aggressors and troublemakers in world peace efforts. This attack will increase and the devil hopes to get the Jews hated by the world and by Christians whose prayers are needed for them. This type of media also wants to portray God as unfair and as having lost control of the world.

The major tool that the devil has used is the tool of evolution. This is a God-denying tool that makes some groups of scientists the new creators of life on earth, allocating to humanity the roles they see fit. This is the most racist of teachings which the devil has used to deceive so many millions of Japheth's children by giving them a false sense of security in themselves. This is the new Babylonian bible written by intelligent people and clever people inspired by the devil.

By reallocating the origin of man to Africa, the evolutionists hope to explain away evidence that points to Adam having been darker-skinned than previously believed. Science has proved that only darker skin could have the genetic variations from which all skin types came. How dark, is not very important. The name Adam also means red earth. By relegating black people to the lowest rung of evolution and the Jews to a not much better position either, Japheth has refused to abide under the tent of Shem like his father Noah instructed him. Satan has also infiltrated the Christian world with his own preachers who mix evolution and the bible. If the evolution human resembled a monkey and had features of "prehistoric" person, that's the evolution's business to explain. Our biblical Adam was created looking like today's man though obviously he must have started as a cave dweller after being expelled by God from Eden and slowly developed from stone tools to iron and beyond. Today we still find some individuals in modern society who do look different and whose skeletons could look 'prehistoric' due to one genetic deficiency or another. That does not mean that everyone else has to look like them just to prove an evolutionary point.

The delusion of evolution is very strong because it appeals to human pride of class, making some colours of people believe that they are more special than Hamites and Shemites. The devil hates Japheth's children who preserved the gospel after the Israelites rejected Christ. Many of Japheth's children died for Christ in the most remote of nations and have been responsible for the salvation of many of Ham's children. It is sad that many of the children of these dedicated Japhethic missionaries have rejected their fathers' gospel of a God who makes all people equal in Christ and have found false comfort in the false gospel of special species in evolution. It is so sad to see how Europe has lost its role of missionary for the Lord and slowly handing it over to others. The hidden treasure of the Kingdom of God is being exchanged for the earthly treasure of the nations.

Racism has become a trap for the mighty nations whom Noah blessed. This witchcraft of Babylon has deluded the strong and subjected them to curses and judgement. It is sad that the Japhethic nations who were blessed to represent God's glory, creative power and might have been deceived by the witchcraft of racism from fulfilling their destiny with justice. The God of Shem, under whose tent they were instructed to abide, is the God whose glory is manifested in love of one's brother. But by 'going in the way of Cain',(Jude vs 11) the Japhethic nations are in danger of giving God's glory entrusted to them to the coming antichrist.

The delusion that God has made those who deny the bible as man's manual for life on earth to believe, is very strong. The simplicity of the bible message has disappointed intellectuals who prefer some jargon-filled encyclopaedias of data. With all the famous books by famous authors filling shelf after shelf of knowledge, man has not been able to find the origin of life on the earth on which we live. Our mountains of writing have simply satisfied the desire of the fruit of the tree of the knowledge of good and evil that Adam and Eve yearned for. Just like them we have missed the fruit of the Tree of eternal life, which is God's Word. No wonder why the written Word on stone tablets (Law) was stored in the ark guarded by images of cherubims (1Kings 8:9&Exodus 25:17-20). Adam and his children would have been kept forever out of Eden and the Tree of Life by a cherub with a flaming sword if Christ had not shed His blood to renew the covenant lost by Adam and allowed them access back to the Tree of life. On crucifixion day, the torn veil to the holy of holies was evidence of our right to return to Eden and to the Tree of Life.

The delusion to continue journeying away from the face of God like Cain is so strong that man continues to feed on the forbidden fruit while access to the Tree of life has been given. And the devil has used the God-given brilliant mind of man to deny God and to recreate a new world order that has no use for God.

The devil deceived the two sons of Noah who their father blessed with the salvation of man and the enlargement of man's knowledge. Most of the misleading intellectual teachings that deny God have come from these two sons of Noah. The descendants of Shem have monopolised world religions and most of it, denying Christ. The image/sign of a lowly Christ did not appeal to their image of a kingly Messiah. Japheth's children, beginning with the Greeks, have sought after things that enlarge the mind's knowledge. Paul says so in 1 Corinthians 1:18-23,"For the Jews require a sign, and the Greeks seek after wisdom."

The quest for man's wisdom has been perfected by the Greeks. To them the whole intellectual world bears reverence. Our bible itself was written in Greek by early translators and Greek has become an integral part of the curriculum in Bible colleges to the extent that some theologians create the impression that those uneducated in Greek are incapable of understanding the depth of the Word.(This may not always be necessary because God made the bible simple enough to be understood by simple people.) The Greeks' poetry, fables, stories, history books and philosophy has kept intellectuals enthralled. Their education system has become the foundation of modern learning handed to us by the Romans. Their quest for wisdom to be like God has led them deeper into deception. They have dangerously identified themselves with the image of Lucifer/Satan to be like God (Isaiah 14). This desperation to be like God has got to the extent where the discovery of a single fossil skeleton is hastily announced on the news with big-sounding words and just as hungrily swallowed without question by viewers who consider it the answer to the missing link to the puzzle of human life. The deception is very strong.

The deception also finds its root in the pride of man. The bible says that God resists the proud but accepts the humble. Before God, those people who are humble or are humbled by circumstances, have a better chance of escaping the delusion than the proud. The devil's original sin came from his pride in his beauty and intelligence. Our world today is obsessed with the desire to be seen as clever, smart, assertive and confident: always to have the last word. The modern world is obsessed with this. That's how the devil is finding it easy to infiltrate our generation. This generation shares the devil's pride in their beauty and intelligence. People who do not look or talk or live a certain prescribed way are despised. Ham's descendants have borne the brunt of this contempt. With their distinct black skin and facial features, they have stood out as different from other nations. The devil has found many willing writers, film directors and preachers who promote lies about them. But just as God judged Miriam with leprosy for promoting prejudicial feelings against Moses' Ethiopian wife in this record of prejudicial reference in the bible(Numbers 12), He will not let those promoting prejudice against black people to continue to get away with it.

But while this delusion grows the truth is also growing. The poor people of this world have found a better covenant that makes them equal to every human being. They have found a Rod of Truth that swallows the rods of the Lie just as Moses' rod swallowed Pharaoh's magicians' rods. This Truth is in a new covenant that a lowly Saviour, who identified with them, brought to earth. This suffering servant Saviour was killed by the Cain-like leaders of Israel. And in His resurrection He redeemed the covenant that Adam had lost. This Saviour is also known as the last Adam.

Chapter 8
The new covenant of the last Adam (1 Corinthians 15:45)

The new covenant by the last Adam is a covenant confirmed by the blood of the Son of Man. He is indeed the last Adam because since His coming, anyone who receives Him becomes a son of God, a greater status than a son of Adam. No wonder why He stated that he who is least in the Kingdom of God is greater than John, whom He called the greatest of all born by man (Luke 7:28). Unlike the first Adam, Jesus overcame the test that Adam failed and denied His will. For the love of His wife, the Church, He was obedient unto death. Adam was disobedient unto death for the love of Eve his wife.

The two testaments

The first Adam had a choice to make. Two testaments were in Eden, the garden of God. One was a testament written on laws determining behaviour and based on human knowledge of good and evil to produce righteousness. This testament could not attain to the level of godliness because no amount of human sacrifice could make them like God. This testament was written on Adam's choice of the tree of the knowledge of good and evil.

The second testament that Adam did not choose was that of the Tree of life that was written with God giving His own life so that man could be like Him. The serpent knew that man wanted to be like God. He deceived him to seek to be like God by the wrong tree. Man ended up with a testament/covenant that was based on laws that like fig leaves could only produce seasonal fruit and partially cover his nakedness while in the process he would need animal sacrifice to cover himself. It was the covenant written on stone hewn by man(Moses).

The last Adam was the covenant not written on stone hewn by man but on the Rock of God that was broken before idolatrous man at Mount Sinai. Through this covenant would man find healing in the leaves of the Tree of life again (Revelations 22). Then man's righteousness would no longer be seasonal but like the Tree of life, would bear twelve manner of fruit, each monthly, the whole year round. That's why the last Adam cursed the seasonal fig tree dry down to its roots/foundation (Matthew 21) before He unveiled Himself to His disciples to eat of His body (the Tree of life) in the upper room. Since then a new covenant of God's own sacrifice has been written for man.

God's eternal wisdom

By allowing His own son Jesus to be born of a woman, in the same way Adam's descendants were born, God glorified the pain of childbearing from a curse to a blessing. The scriptures later say that woman is saved by childbearing (1 Timothy 2:15). Instead of the curse, childbearing has become a covering grace for those women who know God. God ensured that the woman repaid the debt that she owed all creation by creating the last Adam, without man's seed. In this way, she was given the grace to give birth to the Seed by which the Kingdom and dominion lost in Eden would be redeemed back to Adam.

By the thorns on His brow He removed the curse in human sweaty labour and turned the thorny symbol of cursed earth into a crown of glory. He became the curse of all creation and redeemed the former glory of God's creation. In this way this last Adam redeemed the lost kingdom and gave it back to man. Mary Magdalene mistook the risen Christ for a gardener (John 20:15). Maybe she was not really mistaken. This was the resurrected image of Adam, the gardener of Eden. He has since then been calling men to work in the Lord's field. The kingdom that God planted in Eden is not lost: it is back in the hands of God's tenants. And the keys to the kingdom has been given to the church (Matthew 16:19). The keys of life and death are back in the hands of Christ the last Adam.

The last Adam gave His own eternal life to purchase eternity for mankind, which had been lost in the Garden of Eden. The spirit part of man that had died for eating the forbidden fruit can rise again through the process of getting born again (John 3:3) and the garment of glory that they had lost has covered their nakedness. And He crushed the head of Satan and all his plans for mankind.

Just as Adam's side was opened and a rib used to create his bride Eve, so did God allow Christ's side to be broken by a Roman spear to testify the new birth of a new Eve, His church, His body (Ephesians 5:23). He shared the birth-pangs of all women by suffering the labour of mankind at the cross. The redemption of the robber/murderer on His right side was a startling image-redemption of the Cain of the first Adam while the recorded resurrection of the saints (Matthew 27:52-53) was consolation for the memory of Abel.

Jesus became the complete image of the Son of Man that God intended in every generation of mankind. The Abel, who was righteous and was slain by Cain(spear) but whose blood now spoke better things than that of the former, pleading forgiveness for evildoers instead of revenge, the Enoch caught up to heaven, the carpenter Noah who will build the ark of a New Covenant and sail His redeemed over the flood of judgement. He is the new Noah who is husbandman of the vineyard and gave us new wine at the beginning of our marriage to Him as He did at Cana (John 2). And a new Noah whose cross of shame was born by the man from the land of Ham. And this Noah did not curse even when "His sons" stripped Him naked on the cross. He even became the cursed son of Ham, Canaan, cursed for the sins of others, came to live in the land of Canaan and bore the sins that were not His own, to rid Noah's lineage and the whole world of the curse.

He became the restorer of a new unifying tongue by the Holy Ghost at Pentecost to lead His disciples in building a spiritual house unto God (1Peter 2;5). He became the covenant-bearing Abraham, bringing blessings to all nations, the new Isaac who was sacrificed in the eyes of God on that hill, the new Jacob who founded a new people for God by twelve disciples, the new Joseph who was brought to Egypt and fed thousands from the miracle of 7 pieces of food and has stored away12 basketfuls (John 6:13) of remnants for Israel when they shall join Him in the faith by which God has blessed the Gentiles.

He was the new Moses who by miracles, signs and wonders judged the power of the oppressor and leads His people home through the wilderness of trials and temptations: a new lawgiver of one law of love for God and fellowmen. He was a new Joshua, a new Deborah, a faithful Samson, the mighty king David who establishes the Kingdom at Jerusalem, Solomon the Lover, the new Elijah who brings the ministry of fire and the Holy Ghost. He was the weeping prophets, outside Jerusalem, warning of judgement on her (Luke 19:41).

This last Adam was the predominant image of those imperfect individuals that God raised through the ages as testimony of God's unfailing plan for mankind which Satan can never undo. He brought joy to the heart of the Father by redeeming to Him the perfect image of the godhead that they had created at the beginning, so that man can be empowered to take and exercise dominion that he had lost in Eden.

Through this covenant, all who receive Him, God has given them power to become sons of God without discrimination (John 1:12). He allows them to share the blessing of Abraham and of his children. He frees them from the yoke of the fear of Noah's curse and brings them into the freedom of His grace. By Him God's will shall be done on earth as it is in heaven. What is God's will in heaven? According to Revelations 22, it is God living with man in a land of blessings and glory where there is no curse. The curse represented by Babylon is replaced by the blessing represented by New Jerusalem. In the last Adam the claim that the devil had on every family of Adam's descendants has now been invalidated. It is time for Africa and her people to rise up and regain her confidence. Africa's mighty men need to come out of the bushes where they are hiding like Gideon and acknowledge the greeting of the Lord's messenger angel declaring, "The Lord is with thee, thou mighty man of valour."(Judges 6:11-12)

Chapter 9
The sad decline of Africa's confidence

The confidence of a people is a powerful weapon. A nation whose confidence is lost is hanging on an unstable base. Satan has succeeded in maintaining a sustained attack on the confidence of the children of Ham.

The powerful and almost overconfident Cushite, Nimrod, was such an awesome individual that his assertiveness in building a monumental tower to reach heaven impressed God. The bible says God noted that with this kind of spirit, there was nothing that these united, confident, determined and assertive people could not achieve. God broke their confidence by confusing their tongues (Genesis 11:6-8).

Wherever a nation's tongue is confused their confidence and unity is broken. Slavery has been an effective tool in confusing the tongues of individuals. Those who were led into slavery or exile lost their mother tongue and the confidence that comes with it. Wherever they went they became second language speakers of the master's language, often held in ridicule for their accent and pronunciation of the new language. They had to learn the lifestyle of the master and to some, living up to the expected standards of their masters has been more important and fulfilling than finding Christ. This has dented their confidence and identity. Separated from their own people their own children lost their sense of identity as well as culture. Most deviant behaviour has sadly risen from this loss of identity, loss of culture and loss of role model.

As we observed, Ham's children were founders of the nations. Their almost indomitable spirit made them giants in the land. The image of the Egyptians, Lybians, Ethiopians and various Canaanite groups can be compared to the gigantic image of Goliath the Phillistine, who was almost careless/reckless with his strength. He lost to the more scheming David.

After generations as fearsome warrior nations who were hired as mercenaries by emerging powers, Ham's children became victims of their own strength and overconfidence. The more scheming foreign forces bled away their strength by using them against one another to drain the continent of powerful men and women before they could colonise them. Becoming a second or third class citizen in your own country was effective in destroying the confidence of Ham's children. It would take generations of correction before this confidence could be restored.

From the story of Israel's enslavement in Egypt, we learn how powerful enslavement is on the confidence of the enslaved or former slaves. The confidence of Israel was so damaged by slavery that even when they were free they had more confidence in the calf god of Egypt for which they made a gold image than in the God of signs and wonders. They continued to regret leaving Egypt and had no confidence that they could make it without Egypt. The name and image of the Egyptian always struck a code of terror in them. This had the danger of parents passing on this image to their children and forever keeping them subservient to Egyptians. God ended up destroying this damaged generation and grooming a new generation that could believe and fear Him more than their former masters. This pattern sadly repeats itself in Ham's land. A generation of ancestors who are so awed by their former masters and colonisers that their memory or presence strikes terror and ruffles their confidence is in danger of damaging the confidence of their children. God is creating a new generation that is not awed by skin colour or historical advantages. This is a generation that has borrowed its confidence from the Bible. The healing gospel of Christ is restoring this confidence. Africa needs architects who will teach her children to reconstruct their lives by learning to live the Word of God.

Once the power of Ham's children was diminished, Satan used a new tool to destroy whatever confidence was left in them. Using his own preachers with a bible in their hands he blamed the sons of Ham for the curse of their father Ham. Even those preachers who preached a non-racial gospel found it difficult to explain why and how the children of Ham had fallen so low in their status. As the gospel engulfed Africa, Africans have lived to experience the meaning of Samson's riddle to the Phillistines (Judges 20). God has brought sweet salvation out of a dead lion. The enquirers only found the answer to the riddle through Samson's bride. A more faithful bride with the answer is rising in Africa. And her ever-faithful Bridegroom remains the true Judge of her people. But sadly, like Samson, many strong Africans will remain without their vision and be forced to labour in the grinding mills of Babylon before they grow back their hair again and remember to call upon the Lord for His mercy and favour.

As someone who has lived in a colony, I remember the experience as emasculating. In a pattern similar to apartheid, the blacks were relegated to the tribal trust lands and restricted from urban centres. Wages were different by colour and one had to grow up with the concept of a superior white or semitic master, mistress and their children and dogs. The colonial tongue became the tool of dominance and promotion depended on it. Whatever was colonial was supposed to be right and it took many years of conflict before African independent churches were allowed to practise their own ministries. Dr. Ezekiel Guti, one of Africa's spiritual pillars mentions this in his book 'The African Apostle.' He, and many others like him, had to battle foreign based churches backed by the colonial government before their visions could be realised.

Individuals were promoted for spying on their own African brothers and a good African was the docile one. The master was used as reference point in all dialogue: the role model and he could never do any wrong. It became difficult to differentiate between a Jesus who was perfect and Master and a colonialist who also was portrayed to have the same Jesus-like qualities and skin colour. In some African dialects the name for white man was the same for a god. Such was the respect that was accorded colonial power.

Next in line of respect were those who were closer to the master. On those occasions when the master visited the remote tribal lands, he was the subject of woe, with peasants jostling to lay a glimpse on him and respected almost as a god. The reason why liberators of African countries like Nelson Mandela have been revered in Africa is because they challenged an almost improbable situation. It was impossible to imagine the semi-god master getting challenged and brought to the negotiating table by the sons of peasants. The odds were almost unthinkable save for God's time and plan. God would not allow His own chosen people of Israel to wield permanent authority over those under them. He promised Esau that there would be a time when he would grow strong and break Jacob's yoke from his neck. This principle has been replicated the world over.

The damage that was done to the generations that lived under colonialism was significant. Neo-colonialism ensured that the newly independent African states could not be economically independent, depending on "expertise" of the same foreign masters to exploit resources, determine international price and refining the products. The descendants of former colonial servant ended up despairing with black governments that had no jobs or a future for them and the corruption of those who were supposed to have been their liberators who now held hands with their former oppressors and siphoned their loot to foreign banks. With their confidence in the ability of their liberators to prosper them disappointed, these descendants ended up apologising for their hasty liberation and humbled themselves into new voluntary exile to the lands of their foreign masters where they would forever be reminded of their failures to govern themselves. They ended up having to explain why they were coming to the lands of the same foreigners they had sent packing years ago. Such is the riddle of the masterful way in which Africa has been drained of her confidence, that only God shall be able to answer these questions on their behalf. The spirit of greed has proved that it is not restricted to colour or ethnicity. The devil will use anyone he empowers to impoverish the rest.

Movies have also been used to destroy the confidence of black people. Desperate for some role in movies, some blacks have been portrayed as weak, panicky, cowardly in movies. In most movies blacks would be the first to be killed, to flee a battle or to make the wrong move or to be portrayed as the villain to be hunted down and destroyed by the sleek foreign actor or actress. Movies where blacks were portrayed as savages incapable of reasonable judgement were very popular. Black women were honoured in movies for sacrificing their lives for that of the master's child or family. Where obvious black heroism was celebrated, sometimes, foreigners painted as blacks were cast or the cast became predominantly foreign to mislead history. Black heroism was restricted to sport, sensual music and religious fanaticism. Most heroism of blacks like the story of 'To kill a mockingbird' is a story of an appeal for sympathy, an epitome of tragedy. Stories with happy endings rarely featured black heroes or heroines. Even movies by black producers often demeaned their own people by portraying them as foolish and unreasonable traditionalists incapable of common sense in scenes usually set in poor dwellings.

Comedy was used to suppress black confidence. Africans had to live with comedy where they laughed at themselves as humour. Larger than life cartoons teaching young people early to have a low opinion of their own looks and emotional stability were also used. Not many foreigners would find fun in some comedies if they were reversed against them.

One often hears black people discussing very negative pictures of their own black people. While familiarity may breed contempt, it should not breed disgust at one's countrymen. There is a good reason why God allowed us to be born in our communities. Even after God had called Abraham out from his people he still had the sense to get a wife for his son Isaac from the community of his birth. The devil has succeeded in getting some black people to hate their places of birth, hate their black skin and hate the God who created them black. He has made them feel they have to apologise for being black or African. He whispers to them self-depreciating words about their looks whenever they stand before a mirror and drags their confidence down to zero. When Job had been disfigured by his sickness, the devil whispered to his wife to get him to sin against God. She advised him to curse God and die.

How often does the devil repeat this advice to many black people who are beset by one problem after another or who blame their skin for their problems? One often hears cruel words said about God. The devil knows that we will never grow confident as long as we blame God for making us black. He knows that the first step out of a death-like pit of self-remorse is to bless God for what and who we are. When we bless/thank God we live but when we curse Him we destroy ourselves.

God was pleased with the curly hair He gave black people. He looked at the size of their lips and nostrils and saw that they were beautiful to Him. The dark skin he used to clothe them with was conveniently and magnificently made. In every generation people of every skin colour struggle with feelings of inadequacy about their looks, thereby making a single standard of beauty invalid. People of every skin colour need the healing power of the word of God to be satisfied and confident with who they are. All colours of people have individuals who may be described as not good-looking for one reason or another. But God still sees beauty in these people He created.

On the other hand, sexual images of blacks as sexual objects of foreign women fulfilling their fantasies or as brainless sexual studs with nothing other than generous body parts, is almost a self-fulfilling prophecy. God decries his Israelite wife as running after the Egyptians "great of flesh"(Ezekiel 16:26). Boasting of this endowment has led a lot of Africans into misplaced confidence in sexual abilities, reckless childbearing, polygamy and pornography and stripping themselves naked. Pornography is the worst confidence stripper today with those addicted to it suffering from low self confidence. Black women have been the object of sexual fantasies of foreigners as evidenced by the despicable abuse of the legendary Hottentot/Khoi San woman named Venus who was trafficked from South Africa to European countries for show and sexually abused to death by sexual perverts in the 19th Century. The stripping naked of black man and women has led to poor role models, misguided ambitions and unplanned childbearing. Black women have had to struggle for their role as women of status while black men have struggled for a status better than that of a sexual play beast. Married couples today need to change the model of these foreigners for their spouses and see them as men and women of God with a sober and humble call of duty to their new Master.

Evolution has of course put the icing on the cake by reducing black people's confidence to that of the lowest of the human species. Well calculated by the devil to equate man to the image of animals instead of God's, evolution can put the final nail to any hope of the resurrection of black people's confidence. Pedalled forcefully by scientific false prophets, this new Babylonian 'bible' subtly agrees with the Bible that the first man must have been a man of colour in order to give the necessary genetic variations of skin differences today. The Bible calls this first man of colour Adam or red earth. And then the Bible places his origin in the Mesopotamia region. The evolutionists subtly put the first man in Africa in order to narrow the resemblance of African monkeys to the indigenous population. This is a form of dry and dangerous comedy on the devil's part. And the sad reality is that some black people laugh at this humour and accept the same delusion.

Rediscovering confidence

The bible is the tool that black people should use to rebuild their confidence. Anyone who will read the Genesis Chapters 1 to 11 will see a different picture of himself from the bible. While black people have seen themselves through many other mirrors beside the bible, it is time they went back to their Manufacturer's manual which is the bible.

The bible uses a different set of tools to describe confidence. While the world uses some scientifically-tested method of confidence-building to some credible extent, God's way of confidence-rebuilding is a little different. We should go back to the bible to find out how God defines standards.

The word of God defines the beginning of wisdom as the fear of the Lord (Proverbs 9:10).According to the bible those who do not fear the Lord are not wise no matter how smart they sound. Paul calls the method of preaching of the cross of Christ foolishness to the unsaved (1Corinthians 1:18). And that God ordained this apparently foolish method to call man back to Him, "Because the foolishness of God is wiser than men, and the weakness of God is stronger than men," (1Corinthians 2:25.) Those who put their confidence in God may appear weak to the clever children of Babylon but this weakness is stronger than that of man's confidence. Those who put confidence in a cigarette when they are stressed cannot be stronger than those who put confidence in key scriptures of reassurance from the bible.

African people continue to be humbled by the world. While this is tragic in itself, those who come to know the Lord because of these tragedies will forever be grateful that God has humbled them in this way. The camel and needle complex of the well-to-do in this world makes the foolishness of the gospel too narrow-minded for the broadminded (Luke 18:25). That's why God is calling so many souls from the simple people of this world. "For you see your calling brethren, how that not many wise men after the flesh, not many mighty, not many noble are called," (1 Corinthians 2:26.)

Isn't it amazing that the sign of the child born in Bethlehem that the angels told the shepherds about was of a lowly baby in a manger? Anybody looking for a different sign will remain disappointed. The sign of the lowly Christ will be easier to find among the cattle and sheep herders in Africa than the streets leading to Herod's palace. The sign of the lowly Christ will be easier to comprehend among the labourers in the fields than the halls and stadiums of entertainers. The kingdom of God is bringing comfort and confidence to those whom the world has not embraced with its wealth and pride. God will prosper them in His own way.

God's ways are not the ways of men. He does not take directions from United Nations, EU, African Union or the Duma. He is not impressed by the flashy trinkets of superstars who do not fear Him. It does not make sense to the pleasure and publicity-seeking world that God's angels will celebrate a simple cleaner singing a hymnin the back of office while demons celebrate round the meal tables of the spoiled stars indulging themselves in pleasures. God is astonishing in the way He outwits the devil and lost man. He has "chosen the weak things of the world to confound the things that are mighty. And base things of the world, and things which are despised, hath God chosen: yea, and things which are not, to bring to nought (nothing) things that are." Vs 27-28.

God's law of change is by using lowly and base people and events to bring to nothing the highly established human values and systems. He used a baby born in a manger to a simple woman and a common carpenter to upset the religion and lifestyle of the world. The devil has seen this worrying pattern and this could be one reason why he keeps a wary eye on Africa's despised people. God continues His work where the poor people are and uses them effectively to shake the foundations of the strong and mighty. He gives strength to the weak and enriches them with His word.

John in 1 John 5:14 says, "This is the confidence that we have that if we ask him anything according to his will He hears us..." and that we have what we ask for. What better confidence can any people have than knowing that God hears them? To be heard by God is awesome. In a world where it is hard to be heard by your boss, your MP, your senator, president or king, isn't it amazing that the world has in its midst people that are heard by God? And ironically they are simple mothers, young men and women and elderly folk who are not very clever to the eyes of the world. But they have found the communication line to God's throne and He hears their prayers.

In a world where only the smart, the beautiful and the stars are loved, it is strong comfort to know that Jesus loves you just as you are. To go out to work and be treated like a nonentity and yet return with a smile and a feeling of self-worth is a mystery to the world of the proud and compliment-seekers. Those who have tasted the true love of Jesus have a hidden source of confidence this world cannot comprehend. To be loved and valued by the creator is greater honour than any human award. To be assured of an unimaginable future in the afterlife while those who think they should be worthy by virtue of their nationality or status miss it, puts a spring in the hearts of the lowly people of this world.

The biblical concept of assertiveness is based on a hidden strength called faith. These are the wheels on which our confidence runs. This is the quiet power of those who know God. They are confident that when they pray, God hears them and answers their prayers. When they come together they raise a tower of prayer to the gate of heaven. They speak with one new language in the Holy Ghost till God comes down to answer them. He will arise and scatter their enemies. Their confidence is in the Word of God. They have learnt to believe it and live it. Their Bridegroom has washed them with His Word and like a beautiful virgin they reach out to embrace Him!

Chapter 10
"Black but comely"
Song of Solomon 1:5

The present and future role of Africa and her children in world affairs is growing increasingly clear as we read the bible. Based on the rise of spiritual fervency wherever her children are found, it is safe to predict a change in the fortunes of Africa. God's blessing has always followed a people who find Him and who lift their hands of worship to Him. Since God calls Africa "my people" in Isaiah19:25 this promise relates to Africa as well, "If my people which are called by my name, shall humble themselves, and pray, and seek my face, and turn from their wicked ways: then will I hear from heaven, and will forgive their sin and will heal their land." (2 Chronicles 7:14).This is a sure promise to those who have accepted God's salvation through the new covenant of the last Adam. There is no way God will fail to start the healing process in Africa. For those of us who originated in Africa, the burden of prayer for Africa should be a priority. Apostle Paul, who was the apostle to the Gentiles, never forgot his own Jewish origins. He expresses the heavy burden he bore for Israel in Chapters 11 and 12 of Romans. It is my prayer that those of us who know the Lord could follow Paul's example and bear a burden for Africa and black people.

The great love story of Christ and the black bride is conveniently set at the period of Israel's glory during the famous rule of David's son Solomon. This kingdom is described as the best of man's kingdoms and left a lasting impression on Israel's hope in a greater kingdom by a future Messiah.

Solomon's name means peace and its female version is Shulamite. The black bride brings back the memory of Abishag the Shulamite virgin of King David. By comparing the chastity of the black bride to that of the famed beauty of Abishag, the virgin of his late father David (1Kings1:3) who originated from the district of Shulam/Shunam, Solomon bestowed upon the black bride the ultimate honour of virtue. The love dance of two lovers Solomon and the Shulamite with identical names could be what the author describes as the beautiful image of a 'company of two armies', one from the king of Egypt (black bride) and one of Amminadib's chariots (bridegroom)(Song of Solomon 6:12-13). By bringing Abishag into the song, Solomon seems also to play the double role of his shepherd father, King David and his own glorified royalty. Wisdom, psalms and the beauty of love is woven into a song breathed with heavenly Love. And a black virgin is chosen as the heroine of the love story. Solomon himself dwells on her glorified image when he sings of her beauty.

It is easy to miss the beauty and comeliness of African believers because of the often publicised destitution of their communities. When the model of beauty and comeliness has been set by foreigners it is often not well-received when a black bride says, "I am black, but comely, O ye daughters of Jerusalem, as the tents of Kedar, as the curtains of Solomon." (Song of Solomon 1:5). The tents of the Arabic group of Kedar made from black goat skin were well known for their distinct black colour. Verse 6 describes her blackness as being sun burnt (Greek word for Ethiopia). Then she goes a step further to state that her mother's children have been angry with her and made her keeper of their vineyards while her own she has neglected.

Who else but an African would fit this description? An unexplained anger for black people related to Ham's presumed curse and their close role and record in the bible could be one reason. Who else has a vineyard (land) so neglected and underdeveloped than Africa, while her children have laboured in others' vineyards? This is a prophetic image of the bride/virgin of Christ from Africa who Solomon compares to a company of royal horses of the king/Pharaoh of her land (Song of Solomon1:9).They were stately horses of war: the true image of intercessors.

What does He find so endearing about this bride/virgin that the eternal Bridegroom put Himself in the image of Solomon to sing this song with her? While this song is also a song of natural love, God has used the beautiful human feelings of love to convey deeper spiritual issues between Him and His wise virgins who gather in spiritual Jerusalem to be one united Body married to Him. And His significant attention seems centred on this black virgin. He endows His favour upon her. He allows her to share the experience of His own troubled life so that the beauty of her spirit will shine. She should lift her voice and not be afraid to declare that she is loved by the Bridegroom!

There is a song that intercessors sang every time before prayer in Zimbabwe. It was titled: "Dai zvaibvira" (If it were possible)

"If it were possible
I could be like You
Redeemer of my soul
You denied your life for others
May I too deny my life for others?

To be like You
To be like You!
This is the only thing

I desire to be
You denied your life for others
May I too deny my life for others!"

Only a virgin who is used to keeping the vineyards of others more than hers can sing a song like this. Only she can share this honoured role of dying to self like Her Redeemer. She can comprehend why He was a man of sorrows and acquainted with grief because she has shared this experience most of her life (Isaiah 53). Only a virgin who has been rejected like her Redeemer and sold to her enemies can feel His sorrow. Only the virgin who has been stripped naked, lashed and mocked by crowds can share to carry His cross up the hill. Only a virgin who has been hung out high to be mocked and gaped at by the media of the world can share the shame of her Redeemer. Only a virgin who has been asked by the jeering world "Where is your God?" can share the cry of her Redeemer, "My God, my God; why has thou forsaken me?" And it's only the virgin whose body as a people has been buried who can share with Job the hope of rising again. Like him she defiantly answers "For I know that my Redeemer liveth, and that he shall stand at the latter day upon the earth: And though after my skin worms destroy this body, yet in my flesh shall I see God: Whom I shall see for myself, and mine eyes shall behold, and not another: though my reins be consumed within me."(Job 19:25-27). This is that Redeemer who identified with the cursed son of Ham Canaan, was born and died a cursed life in his land. The land of a cursed people has become the centre of blessing for the whole world.

It is often disheartening to find black women questioning their beauty as they measure it against the foreign standard set by foreign media. With a powerful media that controls fashion and beauty, foreign shapes of lips, nose and mouth have been ingrained in the minds of women as the standard for beauty. This has sadly dented the confidence of some black women who continue to struggle everyday with their rightful desire to be beautiful. The word of God is raising a generation of young women and mothers who are growing confident that they are black but comely. They see a world that cannot resist the beautiful shades and hues of black skin that is adorning the nations of the world today. They have learnt to bless the Lord for making them black and have seen Him bless them for being thankful. They have rejected the devil's lie to curse God for their black skin.

The Bridegroom is attracted to the black virgin's smile. Her bubbly spirit lightens the room when she enters it. Her joyful nature makes individuals ask why she is always happy. It has been said of black people that they are ready to smile and easily approachable. Their power has been in their friendly nature, more so when they are born again. Though this virgin has laboured in everyone's vineyard, she bears more forgiveness than bitterness. In a world where people are sour-faced and grumpy, she teaches them to smile again and learn to show the beauty of their spirit. This is the spirit God wants her to impart to a world that is heavy-laden. One well known foreign pastor with a heart for Africa, being interviewed on an African TV channel, said that one could not help but love Africa and her children because of their warmth, fervency and welcoming spirit.

And there is the other face of Africa that many foreigners may never know. It is that face which baffles many who meet Africa's children. It is their resilience against all odds. They seem to have an unbreakable dominance over adversity that amazes many people. Those who have mistaken this warmth for weakness and underestimated them have often regretted it. The devil has never done so and keeps a constant siege on black people.

God is waiting on the interceding black bride to see the hearts of the children of Africa reconciled with those of their fathers. She should have a vision of Africa's displaced children forgiving the land of their fathers for the evil of slavery and exile and reaching out to love the land of their origin. May the Lord use the sad images of African despair to stir the hearts of her children who have found consolation in foreign lands to pray and love their brothers and sisters? The raised voices of prayer from Africa's children all over the world shall bring speedy healing to this vineyard that has been ignored for many centuries. Africa's power is in her prayers; in her unquenchable fire for her Lord. The black bride is called as an intercessor first and foremost.

Black families in both Africa and foreign lands are in crisis of crime and unrequited anger. Inequality both at home and abroad has made them this bitter. They need healing. As the prayers of intercessors from Africa and foreign lands come before God as a united family, God will release healing to our growing children. Africa needs intercessors with the faith that calls down God's healing of the wild storms in the lives of our children.

The power of the cross is the only healing balm for the children of Africa. All bitterness and every burden are healed at the cross. All the generational curses are nailed at the cross. The bride should shout out and declare that there is no curse or witchcraft that can cross the Red Sea of blood after the redeemed children of the kingdom. God is entrusting His bride from Africa to feed the flocks with the manna of heaven, the True Word that is fresh every morning. And it is her ministry to talk to the Rock to provide abundant waters of the Spirit to heal and quench the multitudes. Because she that the Bridegroom chooses and gives living waters, He will send out to tell.

The images of women and children fleeing war, of children with fly-ridden faces, of hungry and emaciated bodies, of endless lines of arms raised for handouts, of disease and of depravity of every kind are waiting for God's brigade of intercessors. These images demean Africa's children in the diaspora who yearn for something better about their motherland on foreign TV. Intercessors are needed who will diffuse the well-fortified field of curses that demons have laid like landmines all over the African land to subject Africa to perpetual shame. Let them stand upon the walls of their motherland and hold hands of faith to ask the Lord who comforts Jerusalem to comfort her children in Africa.

"If you believe and I believe
And we together pray
The Holy Spirit must come down
And Africa must be saved!

And Africa must be saved
And Africa must be saved
The Holy Spirit must come down
And Africa must be saved!"

Africa must be saved from her curse of shame. Africa must be saved from hatred. Africa must be saved from sin. As the song says, when the Holy Spirit comes down, Africa must be saved. God is raising an army in every nation in Africa who will lock into God's will for Africa and like a wheel within a wheel bring God's train of glory into every country. If every one of us who can call upon the name of the Lord will pray God's will in our countries of origin, the devil will find the temperature too hot to operate effectively in Africa. A daily prayer from the often underestimated Lord's Prayer would be a good starting point.

"Our Father Who art in Heaven
Hallowed be thy name
Thy kingdom come to Africa
Thy will be done in Africa as it is in heaven
Give Africa this day our daily bread
And forgive Africa her trespasses
As we forgive those who trespass against us
And lead Africa not into temptation
But deliver her from the evil one
For thine is the Kingdom in Africa

The power and the glory
Forever and ever in Jesus' name."

Africa's daily bread and water has grown into a challenge that needs prayer and intervention of God's kingdom principles. The generosity of the children of Ham has often enriched others instead of them. In some cases it has led to their impoverishment. But for the thrifty, Africa's well publicised problems have become a source of blessing. Charitable organisations, including foreign church groups, are tapping into the generous spirit of black people to raise finance for themselves and for African communities for food, medicine and clean water. Yet sadly, very few black-led churches in foreign lands are driven by the same bowels of mercy projects for their motherland, missing out on this blessing for those who consider the poor. Some sadly spend time gleaning for the widow's mite to further their ministries instead of providing for the widows. May God stir again the hearts of Africa's children to feel guilty for ignoring the daily provisions of their mother's children!

If one man, Daniel, prayed for a breakthrough for His Jewish people until the angel of the Lord brought down to him God's will for his people, how much can we do in our prayer bands? You might be the Daniel that God is raising for your people. Daniel's prayer, made in exile in Babylon, brought about changes hundreds of miles away in Israel in God's due time. Africa needs Daniels who pray through and get God's promise for their nation. Africa is asking her children in foreign lands to pray for her.

God is raising militant brigades from Africa to conclude the original role of Ham in His plan. Ham was the nation builder in man's kingdom. There are very few nations in the world where Ham's children have not been involved in nation building. Whether this was forced involvement or by original plan, Ham has fulfilled his role. God is calling Ham's children to build His Kingdom. The fervency of Ham's children is needed to fire the church. The loud and hearty music of the children of Ham is needed to set the world on fire again. Ham has found the spiritual blessing in Christ that his father had denied him and he is hungry for the things of God.

The powerful music of Africa and natural dance in praise and worship makes her so beautiful to the Bridegroom. She should rid herself of the tired songs missionaries forced upon her. The strongholds of evil, like walls of Jericho, are crumbling before the music of Africa. Strongholds in foreign lands will also fall in the same way. Missionaries from Africa to foreign lands should not discard of their powerful anointed choruses and hymns for some refined but powerless songs of their host countries!

Ham's children have firsthand experience of the power of Satan and make no apologies in hunting, chasing and breaking the power of the devil. They have been humbled by life's problems and find it easy to humble themselves before God. God has taught Ham's children the hard way that He hates those who sit carelessly at ease. While other nations relapse into a life of ease and recklessness, Ham's children do not have much to lose in serving Christ. They are rapidly becoming the most significant missionary to the children of Shem and Japheth. Events on the spiritual barometer show that they are likely to play a leading role in God's assignment to the nations of this world.

God is asking the black bride to raise prayers for the children of Shem who are fighting each other. God asks Ham too to pray for their peace and promises him prosperity for it. Psalm 122:6 says, "Pray for the peace of Jerusalem: they shall prosper that love thee." The destiny of Ham's children and those of Israel and Shem's children appear to be linked just as they were in the bible story. It is critical that the children of Ham who were Gentiles in the Abrahamic covenant but have found God's favour in the new covenant should be humble in their minds.

They have not replaced Israel in God's plan and will not be complete without Israel's children in the Kingdom. It is our duty to pray for the salvation of the children of Israel and other Shemite families who are bogged down in Christ-denying religions. The devil is committed to get them to destroy each other and Jerusalem has become the focus of that conflict. God promises us prosperity if we care to pray for the peace of Jerusalem. Ham's children should not miss out on this powerful promise to prosperity that Japheth's children have already embraced.

A spiritual storehouse of the real bread is being stored in Africa with the hardworking bride of Africa. With her wide experience of working in foreign vineyards she has become a wise householder who "bringeth forth out of his treasure things new and old." (Matthew 13:52). The simple gospel truth with miracles and Holy Ghost power is being entrusted to storekeepers in Africa during these years of plenty. As the world moves towards a famine of the word of God prophesied by Amos in Amos 8:11-12 through the manipulation of the word for personal gain, shall the simple salvation gospel be found in Africa? Shall princes of the Joseph order who can interpret the dark secret dreams of the kings of the nations prophesy the answer to the hunger of multitudes? The responsibility placed on Africa's shoulders dates back to days of Joseph. Princes rising from Africa's children shall feed the nations and many teachers of the word shall descend on Africa to learn from them and renew their faith before going back to feed their congregations. Soon, many teachers who preach 'popular gospels' shall run out of ideas. Their message shall fail to feed the hunger of the crowds who are looking for a proper diet for their souls. God shall expose their tricks and nakedness. A famine of the word of God shall overtake the world. Will Africa be found worthy stewards to open the storehouses of God's true gospel?

Is Africa again meant to be the destiny of some of Israel's children when the antichrist persecutes them? Shall they find a storehouse of spiritual food in asylum in Africa and her deserts? Shall an explosion of revival involving Africa and Israel overtake the world and many of Shem's descendants during antichrist's rule? No one can say with certainty. But it appears like the biblical relationship between Israel and the land of Ham has a prophetic proportion to it.

Together with spiritual food, Africa has again become the destination of a resource-hungry world. God has hidden so much resource in Africa that a new economic highway from Africa to foreign lands is being negotiated to offer both food and other resource security for the future. The warm heart of Africa can be used by God to build societies where foreigners are welcomed and not reviled: societies with a home for us all and developing from the united input of different nationalities dedicated to developing her. It is important for prayers to be made so that Africa does not become the proverbial carcass to which the vultures again descend to ravage her resources.

Africa needs leaders like Jehu to be anointed by prayers. Jehu was a man of action who God instructed Elijah to anoint king over Israel, to bring about swift change in the land. God knew that there were some stubborn dynasties like that of Jezebel which could only be removed by an individual anointed to do so. The action-packed spirit in Jehu was so powerful that the anointing prophet sent out by Elijah's successor, Elisha,(2 Kings 9:8) was told to run away as soon as he had anointed Jehu. Jehu was famous for his furious driving of his chariot and he was a brilliant archer who did not miss with his bow and arrow.

Within a short time he had killed two evil kings Joram and Ahaziah and destroyed Jezebel, the widow of king Ahab and mother of wickedness and demonic worship in the land (2 Kings 9). Jehu followed with killing all Jezebel's sons and destroying their evil dynasty.

Evil dynasties backed by demonic Jezebel power besiege African nations. Through leaders like Jehu, it is expected that God will unleash quick solutions to lingering problems of Africa. But unless God's army of intercessors anoint a Jehu with God-given power to break stubborn dynasties, very little change if any, will be felt in the land. Satan is always ready to anoint another Jezebel to take over unless intercessors step in.

The black bride needs to confront the child of Babylon's witchcraft called racism and bring it down with prayer. This is a formidable spirit but it shies away from the light of day. It falters before the light of the Holy Ghost as she prays to have it exposed. Wherever racism is discerned the believers should go to war against it in prayer and the Word and expose it. Wherever two or three are faced with this racist witchcraft and come together in prayer, God will shake the foundations of this stronghold. While it helps to talk about racism, it is more effective to pray over it wherever it is discerned, at work places and in communities. This witchcraft tool may look strong and stubborn but always flees the light of stubborn prayer and exposure.

Healing and reconciliation in Africa depends on the tears of the interceding bride. God will begin to forgive our trespasses as we forgive our trespassers. The spirit of hospitality that was in Egypt when they welcomed Israel into Goshen will be needed again as God entrusts Africa with feeding nations. God may send God-fearing foreign pastors and business executives to support Africa in her restoration to glory, not as masters or plunderers but as equal partners with a heart for Africa. If they humble themselves, a new commercial highway will be opened between Africa and the foreign world that will significantly bless us all. As God raised a mighty wind that carried the plague of Egypt's locusts into the Red sea (Exodus 10:19), He will respond to our prayers with a mighty wind of change that will blow away the multitudes of 'locusts' that eat away Africa's resources. There is a coming powerful shaking of the political and economic confidence of the developed world that will bring about a sober reflection in relationships between Africa and foreign nations. A significant shift in natural disasters and adverse weather patterns will shake the confidence of many foreign nations used to comfort and security.

Africa signifies the worst of every nation's fears and her troubles have made other nations feel better and lucky. But just as the judgements of Egypt are an eternal reminder of God's judgement on a cruel world, Africa's sad image is a warning to those nations who are cruel to others of judgement in waiting. For example, the almost comical inflation saga of Zimbabwe between 2003 and 2007 was almost ominous of a world economic collapse that followed soon after in 2008. The blood of Africa's children human carnage that entertains TV screens is ominous of things to come to foreign doorsteps! The almost endless list of black misfortune is a worrying test on nations of the world. The temptation that other nations face in their reaction to these often inexplicable misfortunes is almost of apocalyptic proportions. God always visits those who laugh at others' misfortune with misfortune. That is His sad equation on a world that finds entertainment of suffering humanity. Proverbs 27:1 warns individuals and nations that despise others, "Boast not thyself of tomorrow: for thou knowest not what a day may bring forth."

The song of love in the bible remains the song of the Husband, Christ, and his wife the Church. Like Joseph's coat of many colours, torn and covered in blood (Genesis 37:32), His Body encompasses the nations of this world who love Him and are humble enough to lift their hands to Him. That song has in it the words of a black lover of the Lord who says that she was hated by her mother's children, who made her keeper of their vineyards. She laboured for their vineyards that she never had time to develop her own vineyard. But the Husband has been won by her beauty of spirit and love for Him. He is calling her to rise and come away because the time of her winter is ending.

The Bridegroom loves the voice of his black bride from Ham's land. He wants her to take her place at the frontline of battle with her powerful African songs and dance.

The bride from the land of Ham knows what it feels like to be hated by her mother's children. She knows what it feels like to be mocked for her complexion, to be treated as of inferior value than other human life: to be classified as someone who can't be a success or who can't do what others can do. Her Husband is described as there being no beauty in Him that He could be desired. Isaiah 53:2 describes Him "as a root out of a dry ground: he hath no form nor comeliness; and when we shall see him, there is no beauty that we should desire him." (Where all the supermodel portraits of Christ hanging in people's homes come from is anyone's guess!) This bride of His has been assigned, in many generations, to labour and toil in the vineyards of foreigners at the expense of her own motherland. Her own motherland has become the subject of scorn as it remains neglected and underdeveloped.

Will the bride be able to comprehend the love of her Bridegroom? After years of marrying herself to the traditions of her people will she comprehend when He reaches out to set her free? Like the colt that the owners had tied to the stake near Bethphage (Mark 11), will she know when the Master sends messengers to set her free for His purpose? Her heavenly Solomon is not calling her to tribute like a tenant, but graciously to lead her to rebuild her own vineyard. He is waiting to hear her generous giving heart when she says to Him, "My vineyard, which is mine, is before me: thou O Solomon must have a thousand and those that keep the fruit thereof two hundred."(Song of Solomon 8:11-12)

Jesus knows all about his black bride's struggles. He is reaching out to heal her wounded and perplexed spirit with more grace and peace that passeth all understanding. He is the righteous Judge who shall hear her plea for justice and vindicate her against her adversaries (Luke 18:2-6). And in the end she will confidently declare like her Husband, "Daughters of Jerusalem, weep not for me but weep for yourselves, and for your children." (Luke 23:28).Because she knows that beyond this cross of suffering lies a new role, an eternal calling and the fulfilment of her divine destiny.

Chapter 11
Harps upon the willows

When Judah went into exile to Babylon, a sad Psalm was penned by the rivers of Babylon to commemorate this event. The well known 137th psalm has remained the sad reminder of enslavement and subjugation in all generations.

The exiles were so dispirited that they could not sing the songs of hope in a loving and forgiving God that they had known. Instead they hung their legendary psalmist's, David's favourite musical instrument, the harp, upon the willow trees in despondency. This similar scenario has been enacted by African exiles on many rivers of Babylon/exile all over the world.

While some nationalities cannot live with being rejected, God has empowered black people to override rejection and thrive in the land of those who despise them. They are able to say, "Thou preparest a table before me in the presence of mine enemies." (Psalms 23). Dejection has been the story of black people on the slave ships with the roaring waves swearing in their ears, in the plantations with the screaming voices of their brothers and sisters dying into the distance with their tormentors, the brazen sky echoing with unanswered prayers. The story of the despair of Africa's brutalised children can often be heard in Job's cry for a secret place of rest, "..where the wicked cease from troubling: and there the weary be at rest: There the prisoners rest together: they hear not the voice of the oppressor. The small and great are there; and the servant is free from his master."(Job 3:17-19) Yet out of this tortured generation, today stand mighty warriors of the Lord, a seed that would not die but lives to praise the Lord from all islands near and afar where destiny has given them a place to call home.

The story of black people has been characterised with exile and subjugation. Like other nations of the world, black people have erred from the ways of God. Like other nations of the world, they have set themselves up for curses because of their sinful ways. But talking to black people, some with a lot of bitterness in them, you get the feeling that black people feel more punished in this world than other nations who have committed worse atrocities than them. I have talked to black people who are angry with God and cannot forgive the missionaries who brought the gospel to black people They believe that blacks lost their role and prosperity by giving up the gods of their fathers for the God of missionaries who has gone on to reward strangers with black peoples' resources. Therein lies the reason for a crusade among some groups of black people to revive ancestral worship and ancient deities. To these groups, those who worship the God of the bible are traitors of their traditions. This has divided black families and made it very difficult to offer a prescriptive answer for the resurgence of black power and influence. As a Christian I can only offer the prescription that God offers in His word.

It is more painful when black Christians continue to find themselves asking the same questions about their black skin that they asked before they became Christians. It looks like our gospel has missed something in the healing process of the black Christian. Where Jeremiah was given voice to lament the lot of his Jewish people in Lamentations, maybe black Christians have not been allowed to lament their ethnicity without feeling guilty about it. Is there a place somewhere in God's hidden places where black people can conclude the grieving process of their lost generations and be able to ask the questions that nag them?

What is God saying to black people, either subdued by intricate network of domestic and international greed in Africa itself or those scattered as exiles in foreign lands? The mystery of the prosperous wicked who lord it over black nations is felt more acutely by black people who seem forever subdued with disheartening imbalances of world resources. Why does God appear to allow the yoke of subjugation to remain forever on Ham's descendants? Does God really care when black people are treated as lesser people by other ethnic groups? Black people look at the state of their mother continent and feel like giving up on Africa. They ask questions like: Why were we created this way? Why is our skin subject to prejudice all over the world while other nations' skins are almost a passport for them to respect and acceptability? Why were we given all the resources on earth but not the ability to process them ourselves? Why can't our politicians deliver on their promises? Why are we engaged with some of the most vicious demonic forces in the world? When will Africa's problems end and her pride restored?

It is sad that the rise and growing power of the antichrist's kingdom is already felt in the world and acutely so in weaker communities like those of African descent. The powerful and brutal feet of the beast are already known by African nations who have borne the ruthless leadership of the antichrist's messengers. Christians from African nations will tell of experiences where a different kind of enemy dedicated to wearing out of the faith of the very elect already exists. The often almost insurmountable power that stands in the face of Africa's prayers is evidence of the antichrist's spirit flexing its muscles and rehearsing for the final onslaught on the world. It seems that the antichrist power is always either being rehearsed in Israel or Africa. At the fullness of time, and when the antichrist receives his ultimate power over all nations, the mystery of Africa's problems will be understood. Then nations will get a taste of what Africa has been subjected to for generations.

No one can excuse Africa for her failures and it is important for Africa to take responsibility for her shortcomings instead of continually blaming it on others. It is often attractive to blame someone else for our faults. It is so heart-warming to hear a new generation of African leaders who are telling Africa to rise above self-pity and take responsibility of her today to determine a better tomorrow. Our pastors have grasped the importance of giving their people the Word of God as a net they can use to catch the fish that will restore their night hours of empty toil and restore dignity to their labour.

To me as a black Christian, it is so heartening that the dream of God-trusting princes of the black nation like Reverend Martin Luther King is being realised in the state of black people. His dream, based on biblical principles for mankind, reinforces the vision that only through Christ shall justice be given to the suffering people of this world. He is an example of the exiles who refused to hang their harps upon the willows. They refused to stop singing the Lord's song in a strange land. When their captors asked them to sing them one of the songs of Zion, they sang it to them with the fervency of the black man's spirit in it. They lifted the hands of Ethiopia unto the Lord, and towards His high hill in Zion the sacrifice of their praise was given. God was not ashamed too to be called their God. He will not forget the tears that ran down their cheeks as they sang His songs in a strange land. They will share the confidence of the harpist David himself who knew his God and declared,

"Thou tellest my wanderings: put thou my tears into thy bottle: are they not in thy book?" (Psalms 56:8)

When Esau wiped his tears and came to terms with his lost blessing, there were some words of comfort that he heard his father Isaac saying....,"and (thou) shalt serve thy brother; and it shall come to pass when thou shalt have the dominion, that thou shalt break his yoke from off thy neck," Genesis 27:40. Isaac must have been touched by the bitter tears of his son Esau and in faith prophesied a time when Jacob with all the dominant blessing would not be allowed to keep his brother under subjugation. This is God's principle to all the oppressed of this life. The yoke of the mighty will be broken from the necks of the oppressed. The yoke of every dictator shall be broken. The yoke of the greedy merchants of this world will be broken. But the answer only lies in the victory that comes in the name of Jesus Christ.

In Christ, black people have a better comfort than that of Esau. In Christ, black people have found a city of refuge. He is the one who alone wipes their tears and gives them a new hope in His kingdom. His hand is stretched out to receive the black population who are seeking for a new meaning and sense to their identity. What they have lost of the father's blessing they never had in Noah, Jesus is their key to a better blessing. God has revisited the world and renewed the covenant lost by Adam. Since Christ, the Noah covenant and curses no longer take precedence. Those black people who reject Christ choose to remain under the unequal covenant of Noah.

Ham's descendants cannot be expected to excel and reach their potential like Japheth and Shem who received the father's blessing on their lives while they operate under the Noah covenant. That's why leaders like Reverend Martin Luther King who pointed us to the solution of a just world through Christ were true visionaries. The new Adamic covenant through Christ has levelled the playing field and given the descendants of Ham a step ahead of others at Calvary as His cross bearer. Christ is still waiting on Ham to take this role of a friend who bears the burden of His soul to the top of the hill. The children of Ham have a choice to take the role of trust or be careless about it. The rebuilding of nations is once again on Ham's shoulders and he has to rebuild it based on justice. And the rebuilding principles are found in the kingdom of heaven that the last Adam brought to this world. One visionary African psalmist penned a powerful chorus that invokes this vision:

"Simukai tiparidze
Africa!
Zvaishe Jesu Mambo wedu
Africa!"
("Arise, let us declare
Oh Africa!
About the Lord Jesus our King
Oh Africa!")

The angel of Africa must have sung, "Hosanna to the highest: blessed is he that cometh in the name of the Lord!"(Matthew 21) from the African skies on that day that the baby King entered the land of Ham in Egypt on the back of a donkey His mother must have ridden. And angels must have lay prostrate in worship on the day when the eternal voice of the prophet was heard announcing, "Out of Egypt have I called my Son." (Matthew 2:15).They must have seen the new exodus of the whole world beginning from the land of Ham as the deliverer left Egypt for the land of Canaan. And in the footsteps of the King, one day princes would rise out of Egypt. Then Africa would cease to be the image of bondage and evil to be delivered from and become the hope of freedom where even children can find asylum.

God's purpose in exile

In several ways God has allowed black people to be called out of Africa. As we have noticed in the curse of Canaan, what the devil has meant for evil, God turns into a blessing. No one can deny that out of the pain of being separated from their motherland, many blacks in foreign lands have been blessed in exile. Powerful princes of Africa can be seen and heard every day in foreign lands. Like Daniel they have been placed in high office in the land of exile. Like Joseph, they are giving answers to the economy of nations. Like Ezekiel, they are prophesying mighty visions that God calls the world to obey. Like Esther, they stand for the rights of their people to live and not die. God has called them to become a great nation in foreign lands, powerful preachers and nation builders.

Some have been dragged to Babylon by God's own plan to deliver them from the evil of their fathers. He told the exiles of Israel going to Babylon that God would deliver them there. There is no way some individuals could have found the true God in the community they grew up in Africa. God allowed them to be moved into a foreign place where they could reflect and reach the decision to worship Him. To them, circumstances in exile made them see their need for Christ.

Some have been unwilling but very gifted messengers of God who, like Jonah, had to be forced to go to foreign lands to warn of God's impending judgement. They were so bitter with the foreign nations who had either plundered their lands and done atrocities like Nineveh had done to Israel. And like Jonah they would never imagine praying or preaching repentance to such nations. But God has crushed their businesses, ministries and prestige till He has broken every resistance in them and spewed them into Nineveh. In Jonah's case God assigned his own living submarine, a whale, to transport him. They have learnt that God is a gracious and forgiving God who wants to save those that despitefully use us. They will only return to their land when God has finished His work with them and after they have set up massive revivals in the foreign land.

God even has a purpose for the youngest child who could be trafficked to a foreign land. Sad though it sounds, a little Jewish slave girl in Syria brought God's power of healing to the Syrian palace. She told the king about Elisha, back in her homeland. Namaan, the King's leporous general ended up healed. Intercessors should pray that God uses Africa's children who are trafficked all over the world to glorify His name and be the small thing that awakens the knowledge of God wherever they go.

Just as the Jews going into exile in Babylon had 'prophets' lying to them that God would return them from exile quickly, some African exiles have believed the same. But the truth was that God wanted them to build homes and settle in Babylon because the exile would be long. He even told them to pray for the peace of the land of their exile.(Jeremiah 29:4-9) He blessed them there and gave them an inheritance in foreign lands. When God's time was up, he raised Ezra and Nehemiah to lead those who wanted to go back home. God will speak with a clear voice to prayerful exiles when it's time for them to return to Africa. Complaining, cursing and denigrating the host country is missing God's plan. We should learn to be humble and grateful to God for our hosts and as Paul and Peter instructed, we should learn to pray for our host governments (1Timothy2:1-2 and 1 Peter 2: 13-17).

When God intended to divide the kingdom of Israel, after Solomon's sinful rule, he chose Jeroboam to go into exile in Egypt (1 Kings 11) as a king in waiting. He was in asylum in Egypt until the time was right to move and claim his throne. God has also allowed government changes in Africa in the same way. Many stable governments in Africa bear gratitude to some foreign land that gave asylum to their leaders and educated their technocrats. Africans should pray for foreign lands that have given them asylum and a new beginning in their lives.

When Jacob blessed his children at the beginning of their exile in Egypt, he made one blessing that glorified the dignity of labour. Those black people who can claim the blessings of the children of Abraham can know that God has ordained paid labour as a blessing. "Issachar is a strong ass couching down between two burdens: And he saw that rest was good, and the land that it was pleasant: and bowed his shoulders to bear, and became a servant unto tribute."(Genesis 49:14-15). To Jacob, his son's strong, big body frame was a God-given advantage. By his strength Issachar would be enriched.

The honour of servanthood

The bible story of dying to self and of servanthood is built on the foundation of the curse of Noah. Canaan was cursed to be servant of servants, but as we have observed, his curse was made into a blessing for the whole world. God only raised Joseph into authority after allowing him to experience slavery/servanthood. He only raised his chosen nation of Israel after subjecting them to slavery/servanthood in Egypt. Jesus taught that the way to greatness was by the pathway of servanthood. He, Himself, became a lowly servant, cursed with slavery under the Roman occupying force at the time and died the death of a cursed man to redeem man. Paul called himself a slave of the Lord. By being asked to deny ourselves, kneeling and worshipping, we are reduced to slaves/servants of the Lord. Bearing the cross in our lives is evidence of servanthood. The Lord laid that cross on the shoulder of the man from the land of Ham to emphasise this role. Fasting and praying for souls is evidence of servanthood in labour. What looks like a cursed existence in this life is blessing before God. Slavery/servanthood has an accolade of honour in God's kingdom.

The experience of exile

The process of exile by which God is moving Africans around the world has often been painful. But there is a hidden purpose in His plan. He has not lost control. He is going to repay the aggrieved nations that have been subjected to servanthood. Since to everything there is a season and a purpose under heaven, therefore the season of servanthood will be followed by the season of blessings and honour. The neglected vineyard of the black bride shall flourish and bear abundant fruit and her Bridegroom shall come and rejoice in her delicacies (Song of Solomon 5: 1). That is what God's word says of every purpose under heaven.

The experience of exile itself has had a lot of ups and downs for many Africans. The downside has seen someone's enemies pursuing them into exile. The Jews in Shushan had an ancient enemy pursuing them into the king's palace during the days of Esther. Haman the Agagite, from the remnant of their bitter enemy tribe that God had instructed the disobedient king Saul to wipe out, now reared his head to plot their annihilation in exile. Some Africans will tell of similar experiences either on physical or spiritual levels where their enemies will prepare a gallows/hangman's noose for them like Haman did for the Jewish leader Mordecai. But they need to find comfort that the God they believe in will always raise an Esther who will touch the heart of the king and save them from the enemy. The gallows he had prepared for Mordecai ended Haman's own life. The decree he had deceived the king to make for the annihilation of the Jews ended up turning into a decree to annihilate the enemies of the Jews. Their enemies had dug a pit and fallen into it themselves!

Tests by fire and by the lion's den awaits some Africans in exile as it did for Daniel and his three friends in Babylon. Enemies of the Lord raised strong accusers who kept an eye on everything they did to get them in trouble with authorities, to embarrass them and to destroy them. They found themselves living among people who hated God, hated the way they worshipped their God and hated their confidence in their God. Their accusers get some Africans into jails, inquiries, injury, and life-threatening attacks because of their faith. But God will deliver them from the fire of their fiery trials and comfort them with the strong hand that saved Daniel and his friends.

The exiles who sat by the rivers of Babylon were an assortment of characters. God had judged them for the sins of their land by sending them into exile. The guilty and the innocent were here together. The prophet Ezekiel and the false prophets were here. Thieves, liars and adulterers were here too. Some were hoping the exile would erase their evil past, their crimes, their debts. But they all shared one thing. They all remembered their homeland: the rivers, the hills, the familiar crowds, and the beautiful sunset. Their hearts sang a song of love for their homeland and recalled the enticing verse of their childhood. They share the emotions of every exile to this day that one captured in free verse:

> "It is the song of my home
> Calling out of the open country
> Sweet as the savannah where I grew
> Where the cicada cries in his lungs
> Among the sprawling mopane leaves
> Where the woodpecker pecks unceasingly
> Rattling the young woods to echo
> In tune with the tireless cicada."
> His verse sums up the emotions of those who sat by the rivers of Babylon for whom
> "Shade by shade
> Every memory grows
> Till every shade becomes a memory
> And every memory an emerging shade." (From 'Shades of memories')

Memories always flood those in exile. They continue to be reminded that they are in a strange land. A land where they are reminded that they are migrants and unwanted. But their songs keep them strong in the Lord. They have found Him who said, "Foxes have holes, and the birds of the air have nests, but the Son of man hath not where to lay his head," (Matthew 8:20).They know what it is to be homeless, and in the moonlight to sleep like wayfarers in foreign jungles where lions roam the highways.

No amount of abuse will silence the harps of black exiles who know Jesus. Even if their captors will not ask them to sing one of the songs of Zion, they will do so by the rivers of Babylon. Though their tears will flow like the willow branches where they sit and mirth won't be found in their hearts, their indomitable spirit will keep them believing in the God who is always in control. And even in death they can still be heard crying out like their Redeemer, "Father into thy hands I commend my spirit!" (Luke 23:46).

Chapter 12
Highways to exile

The history of African exile in foreign lands can be traced to the history of early man itself. After that we will get a semblance of exile through God's mirror of nations, Israel. As for the more recent exiles, we shall refer to contemporary and current causes.

An understanding of human behaviour will suggest that the repugnant evil for which God destroyed the Cain generation must have included human trafficking. Man will always sell his fellowman for a good price. If for some reason he can't sell his own kind, he will sell a stranger. Since Cain's obvious disregard for the value of his brother, Abel's blood, man has shown little evidence that the blood of humans is precious. We are sadly moving towards the point where animal life is growing more precious than human life when there should be no reason for such comparison of God's beautiful but different creations.

The first record of a sanction to enslavement is when Noah cursed Canaan to perpetual subjugation by his relatives. It is probable that the first slaves must have come from Canaan's children. But anyone who knows human beings will understand that they rarely keep to boundaries. The bible record is full of evidence that slavery was freely practiced across all colours and all nations.

The first record of slavery we have in the bible is of Sarah's black slave girl, Hagar. In what might have been part of the compensation that Pharaoh had paid for lusting after Abraham's wife, Hagar might have been part of the booty. But what is interesting is that she was already a slave in her own African home. Therefore slavery was already accepted and practised in Egypt. And the fact that she remained a slave in Abraham's home before and after birthing Ishmael, shows that the Hebrew group found nothing unusual about slavery. Hagar is an example of a young woman torn from her African family but ending up as the mother of the Arabs, one of the greatest nations alive today.

The next record is that of Joseph who was sold by his brothers to Hagar's great grandchildren, the Ishmaelite traders on their way to Egypt. Here was recorded evidence that slavery was not reserved to Ham's descendants only. Human beings by nature of their greed, were not likely to keep away from a profitable business like slavery. In an almost subtle exchange, Africa gave Abraham Arab children and Abraham's great grandson Joseph was given back to Africa. Joseph had no curse over him in order to go into slavery. The curse was the greed and hatred of his brothers and the profit motive of the Ishmaelites. The Arabs were one of the earliest slave traders of black people, if not the most involved over the centuries. Millions of blacks are found in Arab lands today.

The record of Israelite enslavement in Africa was further evidence that slavery was not restricted to one group of people. Their enslavement was also God's plan for the grooming of His chosen people into a great nation in Egypt. Africans showed themselves to have been active in slavery. Most of the outstanding pyramids are attributed to this slavery and subsequent enslavement of other nations in Egypt. It was not a curse that sent the Israelites into slavery. It was the greed and hatred of the Egyptian that caused them to turn in this way on their guests. Egyptians, with their massive backup of strong

African armies, enslaved many nations including fellow African groups.

Israel was the mirror of the nations of the world in God's eyes. What happened in Israel and how God reacted to it, was/is a message to the nations of the world of how God deals with them. The record of Israelite enslavement and subjugation by many nations is well recorded in the bible. Most of it was because of their disobedience. However, we can safely assume that the behaviour of Israelite people was no different from the behaviour of other nations. Though God treated Israel differently due to their elect status, He has shown consistency with His blessing and punishment for good or bad behaviour of nations. The prophecies that are made about different nations by prophets in the bible show this. It is important at this point to conclude that slavery was not only reserved for Ham's children and that one did not have to be cursed to be a slave. The unwritten record of other nations would show nations enslaving each other at every given opportunity.

Reasons why and how individuals or nations went into exile can best be summarised as forced exile, circumstantial exile and economic exile. Hagar's and Joseph's exile were forced. The Israelite exile in Egypt was both circumstantial and economic due to the 7 years drought. We shall see how highways into exile to date have followed these patterns. And also how some peculiar kingdoms have devised systems of employing these methods to ensure that exile would remain a tool for exploiting resources and ready human labour. This system was first perfected by the Chaldeans of Babylon and has remained in force since.

From time immemorial, millions of black women like Hagar have been forced into exile by traffickers and relatives especially from north and east Africa into Arab lands and India where their beauty was renowned and where sheikhs married many wives. Some became mothers of dynasties especially in some Arab states where they were accorded status by their husbands. Solomon is an example of one such ruler who desired black women. A similar obsession with black women was also common in West African slave trade and slave ranches in the Americas.

The story of the prophet's widow (2 Kings 4) during Elisha's day is another example of potential forced exile. The widow cried to Elisha that because of her deceased husband's debt, the creditors were demanding the sale of her sons into slavery to pay the debt. The well rehearsed miracle of borrowed vessels that were needed for the continuous flow of oil saved the sons from slavery. This type of exile was common in Africa as well as in traditional societies. The earliest records of slavery in Africa were about debtors, troublemakers, witches and undesirables in society before this dried up and the demand grew. Then brother turned against brother for profit.

Other examples of forced exile were the exile of Israel to Assyria and later to Babylon. The other was the Egyptian and Ethiopian exile to Assyria which was extensively prophesied by Isaiah in Isaiah 20 followed by Egyptian 40 year slavery to Babylon(Ezekiel 29)and the great pains of Ethiopia which followed it (Ezekiel 30:9). All these prophecies were fulfilled swiftly and without undue delay as God ensured that the generations that had sinned did not get away with their sins long enough for them to be passed on to their children. God has shown fairness and consistency by limiting judgement for the sins of the fathers to third and fourth generation children. What was common though about these exiles was that they were God's just judgement for the nations' sins.

Jacob's exile fits into the pattern of forced and economic exile brought about by the need for asylum. Though this asylum was within God's plan, the human element of transgression triggered it. Jacob is an example of some recent exile. Foreign lands have become the haven of individuals who seek asylum from crimes they have committed in Africa. Some flee with their friend's spouse, flee embarrassing debts, thefts, false promises etc. Some impoverish their families to raise airfares and like Jacob are not keen to meet their victims. Like Jacob many have nothing at the port of entry into the foreign country and claim asylum on false pretences. They are voluntary exiles ready for any job available. Like Jacob they find God's blessing in the foreign land and become a powerful family. Jacob's character and circumstances fit that of the modern African exile. No wonder why he is the father of Joseph, the role model to Africa and why he brought the patriarchal blessing to Africa. Highways into exile have not always disadvantaged Africa and many individuals should reflect soberly on this and heed God's command to pray for their hosts.

Babylon perfected the art of bleeding nations through forced exile of the intellectuals, the well to do and those with skills needed in Babylon, leaving the poor and incapables in the land under an appointed leadership. Therefore Babylon ensured that they removed the king/prime minister/president they did not like and replaced him with another citizen of the subdued land who was loyal to Babylon and would ensure Babylon exploited whatever resources the land had left. The country slowly grew weaker and poorer forcing the remaining citizens to seek voluntary exile. This was the case with young intellectuals like Daniel who were carted to Babylon and ended up in leadership roles there. Their king Zedekiah was deposed and taken to Babylon where he was blinded and his children killed (Jeremiah Chapters 39 and 52) while a puppet king was left in Jerusalem. A few years later another group of exiles that included prophet Ezekiel, was to follow.

Those who remained in Jerusalem were poor and hungry. Together with the prophet Jeremiah they went into voluntary exile in Egypt. They became economic migrants in Egypt. While those who went to Egypt ended up unstuck when Babylon brought to an end Egyptian power in the world soon afterwards, those who had gone to Babylon either grew quite rich and well settled away from home. Even after the 70 years of exile, few returned to rebuild Jerusalem. Babylon ensured the end of the world power houses of the day in this smart way. The names of the kingdoms of Israel/Judah, Egypt/Ethiopia, Assyria/Syria remained as occupied territories of new submerging powers, never to have a king again from their original founder people. Leadership in their lands today does not appear to originate from the founder people.

The systematic manner in which Babylon perfected the art of empirical control could well explain why the vision of the human figure that Nebuchadnezzar got interpreted by Daniel identified him as the head of the new and final dynasty of nations. The new generation of kingdoms that would rise would be led by the same style of control. Future highways into exile would be paved on this Babylonian pattern.

Africa has been the focal point of the Babylonian style of subjugation. After the initial slave trade in unwanted individuals from their societies, the real trade involved the bleeding of some of the most able people from Africa to foreign commercial fields. Many have remained in their new adopted lands. Some have grown very rich and settled but some have done poorly. Some have made their way back to Africa and tried to rebuild their lives. Over the years, the weakened African communities were colonised and at the end of colonisation, loyalty to the former colonial powers remained crucial for development aid and access to world trade. The unabated outflow of resources from Africa and impoverishment led to economic exile into many foreign countries. Today, many African Daniels are intellectuals in foreign lands. Many Ezekiels are prophesying in the diaspora. Many Jeremiahs are wondering why they are prophesying from a place like Egypt which they warned others not to go.

The vacuums that were created in Israel by the removal of communities created an influx of new groups of people claiming land and property: for example the mixed group of Assyrians and Jews (from intermarriage) called Samaritans, the Edomites and remnants of Canaanite groups began to vie for control of the land with the remaining weakened Jews and even resisted those who later returned with Nehemiah and Ezra (Nehemiah 5). God's promise ensured though that the return would succeed. However, in Africa, the power vacuums have created a lasting menace of tribal wars of claims and counter claims to territory. The reckless spirit of hunting and selling of fellow Africans has led to a breed of lawless individuals whose only means of livelihood has remained the guns their grandparents inherited in trading away their brothers and sisters. Africa's present sorry state seems more related to the greedy manipulation of the Babylonian system that has led many of her children onto the highway to exile more than to the prophecies of judgement, the Israel enslavement in Egypt, or the alleged curse of Noah on Ham. The highways to exile are mainly man-made and devil driven. Thank God for His damage-limitation grace that follows His people in exile.

Exile in any form remains a painful experience. But the God who can make all things work for good for those who love Him is ready to turn what should be a curse into a blessing. Today, massive numbers of exiles gather every weekend to find consolation in one another and in Christ as they worship Him. They find time to talk with nostalgia about their homes far away and encourage one another about a better day coming for their people: the day when they will pack their belongings and return to their motherland. And even as the years go by and their dream remains unfulfilled, they sing in joy and talk about the God who rules in the affairs of men. And by His grace, they know that one day the highway to Africa will be congested with her children returning with blessings in their hands. Maybe the day is not very far off when calamities in foreign lands shall drive Africa's children back to their motherland in a pattern similar to that of Israel's return to their land in recent times.(Further understanding of what Babylon is can be found in reading of Notes Chapters 3 and 4).

Chapter 13
"Comfort ye, comfort ye my people," Isaiah 40:1

I listened to a great man of God prophesying comfort to the children of Africa. He was prophesying to a country that was economically down on her knees. Violence and uncertainty gripped the nation and she had become the laughing stock of the world. Corruption had become a way of life and life expectancy was at its lowest and basic services had wilted. At face value one would not tell which African country this was. Why? Because this picture presents itself in many African countries and the voice of comfort for one is the voice of comfort for the rest.

A concerned individual who visits to share in Africa's sorrow may find themselves in the same position of Job's friends.

"And when they lifted up their eyes afar off, and knew him not, they lifted up their voice and wept; and they rent everyone his mantle, and sprinkled dust upon their heads toward heaven. So they sat down with him upon the ground seven days and seven nights, and none spake a word unto him: for they saw that his grief was very great." (Job 2:12-13).

"Speechless", is often the word used by the many concerned individuals who have seen for themselves and tried to offer personal and close comfort to African communities. And such many comforters have visited and tried to comfort Africa's children in their own best ways. But their best efforts have sometimes been interpreted as accusatory, judgemental and patronising. Job said of his comforters, "Miserable comforters are ye all," (Job 16:2). How would Africa's comforters feel if the same was said of their sterling efforts? There was something that Job's comforters missed in their comfort. Maybe Africa's many comforters also miss the same point. Job wanted to make sense of his suffering. He was looking for a Redeemer who would raise him up again. That is what Africa also needs.

Africa needs friends with the sensitive wisdom of young Elihu, to challenge the often self-righteous pleas of her people. The great man of God I heard prophesying was calling the weeping and suffering nation to own up to their own shortfalls before God, reach out and touch Jesus Christ. He knew that once they found Jesus their questions would be answered and that He would hear them and redeem them from their fears. With Him they could sail through the flood of troubles and stay safe in the ark.

Africa has a lot to thank the Japhethic nations for. When the Israelites stalled in their call to bring Christ to the nations and when the gospel to the Gentiles that had trickled through North Africa and Ethiopia had dried up, Japhethic messengers from God came to Africa. Though they were like the voices of one crying in the wilderness saying, "Prepare the ways of the Lord!" and many of them with a gospel that was based on water baptism, they were forerunners to the gospel of fire and power that has overtaken Africa today. They pointed Africa to Him who was coming to Africa "through the tender mercy of our God: whereby the dayspring from on high hath visited us (them), To give light to them that sit in darkness and in the shadow of death, to guide our feet into the way of peace,"(Luke 1:78-79).

Jesus, the dayspring from on high, indeed visited Africa physically as a young child. The Prince of peace found peace from Herod in a land that yearns for peace. He will indeed lead the Africans into the way of peace that they cry for if they welcome Him again. And Japheth's worthy sons and daughters who have been faithful to the dream to see Africa arise and shine will rejoice with her children. Some have remained dedicated to Africa and toiled for black people to see the birth of princes of the Kingdom and selflessly given way to see them increase in stature. They remain worthy partners on the African battleground and have touched the black disciples' visions with the mantle of their own dispensation.

Therefore no one can take away from these Japhethic missionaries their John the Baptist wilderness call in Africa. Though many of their fathers did not baptize Africa with fire and the Holy Ghost, they were a burning light and our fathers came to their light for a season. They laid the cornerstone of missionary centres, educated many African leaders and laid fundamental Christian values that have shaped the conscience of many people in Africa.

Incidentally, some African nationalists blame some early missionaries for opening the door to plunderers of African resources. This seems to agree with what Christ said to his disciples that where the carcass is, there the vultures will be (Matthew 24:28). Many false teachers and imperialist missionaries made merchandise of the gospel in Africa and attracted mercantile vultures who fed on the dead gospel they propounded. The curse of Ham and its racial tone was an example of such dead gospel. Like all false gospel that attracts fortune-seeking vultures, the scent of the meat coming from Africa attracted foreign vultures to exploit African resources.

However in the fullness of time, God has raised princes in His kingdom in Africa who have taken the mantle to higher levels. Anyone who has kept an eye on the spiritual awakening of giants in Africa will tell of massive miracle and wonder ministries taking the kingdom for the Lord with violence (Matthew 11:12). They have shaken the foundations of the devil's kingdom and are sending warriors to many lands to fight battles for the Lord. Africa has been renowned in history as the source of the most terrible of mercenaries by foreign nations. And today, terrible Kingdom warriors are rising out of Africa and joining ranks with the armies of the Kingdom in foreign lands. The world will rejoice at the sound of their marching feet: the enemy camps will tremble.

God is comforting Africa with the rise of Holy Ghost power-filled princes who know God and their power over Satan's kingdom. And these princes are going after the groves of the forests of Africa similar to the ones of Ahab and Jezebel during the days of Elijah. They shall bring down the shrines and high places of the gods of the land and set them on fire. A double anointing of power that breaks every yoke shall be upon those like Elisha who He will touch from the fields. They are shepherds who come after the line of God's shepherds Abel, Abraham, Isaac, Jacob, Moses and David. They are the shepherds that carry the angels' good news of a Child born in Bethlehem of Judea whose name shall be called, "Wonderful Counsellor, The Mighty God, The everlasting Father, The Prince of Peace" to Africa! (Isaiah 9:6).

Jesus is reaching out to the inhabitant of Africa who bore His cross up to the top of the hill and whispering to him, "Your burdens are lifted at Calvary. It is I, fear not!" Jesus is sailing the stormy sea with Ham to the demon-besieged shores of Africa where legions of demons have shackled the mighty of the land, who are screaming to the four corners of the world. Jesus has an appointment with Africa and will rid the land of the cursed thing.

And to the exiles who sit by the rivers of foreign lands singing, "Come by here my Lord: Come by here!" (Kumbaya) God wants them to know that He has heard the voice of their lamentation and bitter weeping just as He heard Rachel's voice. He has already promised, "Refrain thy voice from weeping and thy eyes from tears: for thy work shall be rewarded, saith the Lord: and they shall come again from the land of the enemy. And there is hope in thine end, saith the Lord, that thy children shall come again to their own border." Jeremiah 31:15-17.They shall again lift their hands with their brothers and sisters from the south of Africa to the north, east and west of it to sing:

Nkosi Sikelel iAfrika (God bless Africa):

God bless Africa
Let her name be lifted high
Hearken ye to all our prayers
Lord bless us
Even we, her family!
Come Holy Spirit
Come Holy Spirit bless us! (Own translation).

It is the prayer of the black bride saying, "Awake, O north wind; and come, thou south; blow upon my garden, that the spices thereof may flow out. Let my beloved come into his garden, and eat his pleasant fruits."(Song of Solomon4: 16)

When Jesus cried, "I thirst," at Calvary (John 19:28) the Romans gave him vinegar to drink. And similar oppressors have given exiles 'vinegar' when they thirsted. But Christ shall comfort them with living waters when they cry out in their thirst. God shall not forget their labour and the tears of their toil in slave plantations and colonial mines. He is the God who rewards His people for their suffering. They shall rejoice when their children take their high places in the world and bring change and justice to the nations. It is His season to turn their much toil and labour into rivers of blessings.

The lost generations of Africa's children shall not be forgotten before God. Those who like the lost coin lie in the dirt of the streets, in the garbage heaps and in the forgotten places of this earth, God will gather. Though they may be rated as cheap as a penny, the lowest of the nation's currency, the Creator treasures them. He is sending the woman (His church) with the light of the Holy Ghost to sweep for them in all the dark corners, recover them and bring them with rejoicing to Him. They are His precious coins and His image is stamped on them.

God will comfort Ham with the promise He gave to Israel. As He gathers the scattered of Israel, He will turn the hearts of Ham's exiled children to remember their nations of origin. He shall stir their hearts to remember the destitution of their land. They shall cover the nakedness of their land with beautiful buildings, infrastructure and a new beauty. A new landscape is rising in Africa as her children in exile jealously endow her with the blessing of their foreign labour.

There is a new world of Africa hiding in the media bushes. Africans have been blamed for living hidden in the forests of their continent. Ironically, there is an Africa of exquisite beauty and unsung excellence that the media has hidden away. The landscape of Africa is changing daily. Beautiful homes, luxurious neighbourhoods and clean villages are rising all over the land. If a cameraman chose for a change to divert from his normal photo-shoot of the shanty towns of Soweto and went into Protea suburbs, left the road that goes to the slams of Mbare (Harare) and chose the suburbs of Wesgate or instead of the slums of backyard Lagos and chose the view of Victoria Island!

A visit to the villages wouldn't be disappointing. The 'normal' pole and dagga dwelling is no longer fashionable in Africa and has not been so for decades. Every child who can make it to the city or overseas is prepared to die trying to change that sorry image of his ancestors' dwelling. Africa's children have a vision of an Africa that is different, that reflects their proud origin.

God shall join the hearts of the sons of Africa to the house of David with an everlasting love: just as He did with the heart of Jonathan. Jonathan's father, Saul, went seeking the oracles of mediums at the caves of Endor,(1Samuel 28:7) just like our rebellious fathers sat before the mediums of the forests and hills of Africa. But Christ has ensured that we shall not die for the sins of our fathers like Jonathan. He has made us the mighty ones who will not fall but shall live and declare the works of the Lord.

In Christ we have found more grace and it shall be said of us "..very pleasant has thou been unto me : thy love to me was wonderful, passing the love of women" 2 Samuel 1:26. Christ has made us to retrace the steps of our ancient friendship with Israel and to pray for the peace of Jerusalem. Though some Christians feel that some Israelites do not treat them with respect or warmth they should love them and pray for them for the sake of Jerusalem. For without the harp of David in our rejoicing, our joy will not be complete.

As Egypt remains a wonder to the world and the architecture of her pyramids a mystery to all generations, so is God raising architects in Africa who shall build ministries that shall astound the world. The world shall come like tourists to Africa to learn of the mysteries of God's power and glory. For He is raising princes in Africa who, like architects, are endowed with outstanding skills, wisdom and power. They are giants in the land, men and women of renown. Her children in foreign lands have become powerhouses of the treasures of the Lord's kingdom and their voices are loud and clear over the airwaves and satellite stations all over the world.

As his father Jacob comforted Joseph with this blessing, so shall God comfort Africa and her children, "The archers have sorely grieved him (Joseph), and shot at him, and hated him: but his bow abode in strength, and the arms of his hands were made strong by the hands of the mighty God of Jacob..."Genesis 49:22-26. By divine appointment Jacob brought the father's blessing to Africa. Egypt received Jacob/Israel as their own father. Israel went before Pharaoh and blessed him. This love and reverence was renowned by the grievous 70 day lamentation of the Egyptians when he died. So sore was their funeral mourning that the Canaanite tribes were shaken by it. "They said, this is a grievous mourning to the Egyptians: wherefore the name of it was called Abel-mizraim, which is beyond Jordan." Genesis 50:11.The use of Abel is significant of the eternal cry of Abel's grieved blood. God has not forgotten the eternal cry of Mizraim (Egypt) the children of Ham, for their spiritual father Jacob/Israel beyond the river Jordan.

God promised to call them beloved that were not beloved. Jesus told the Pharisees that God would raise new children for Abraham. And it is quite obvious that from all the places where Abraham's feet walked, from Mesopotamia, Egypt and Canaan, the promise is being fulfilled. Through Christ, Africa will be comforted in Abraham's bosom and at the breasts of Sarah who is their mother Jerusalem (Galatians 4:21-27).

The first song that I heard at my mother's knee and which I loved to sing at our African school assembly was:

"Jesus loves me this I know
For the bible tells me so."

At a young age I learnt of the message of love that the bible had for me. It is the same message of comfort children of Africa should read. In a world of racial feelings and hatred, it is sweet to know that Jesus loves an African child with a mucus-covered and fly-infested face and the load-bearing destitute woman fleeing gangs of militants. That He loved them so much to die for them and to assign angels who keep a record that their blood will one sure day be accounted for before Him.

God is raising mighty hunters before His face in Africa. They will hunt after every demon in the land and build a tower of prayer to the Lord. They are powerful intercessors, their brother's keepers, who will speak with one tongue before the Lord. They shall go after the precious soul and bring it as a present before the Lord in Zion. And He shall not scatter them there but He shall call heaven to witness the power of their heaven-shaking faith and nothing shall be restrained from them. He shall rejoice when the violent sons of Ham take the Kingdom by force. And with their nets they shall fish for souls from the troubled seas of the nations.

Isaiah heard the Lord saying, "Comfort ye, comfort ye my people, saith your God. Speak comfortably to Jerusalem…" He saw the comfort reaching out to those who were not Israel. And Ham was one of them "Whom the Lord of hosts shall bless, saying, Blessed be Egypt my people, and Assyria the work of my hands, and Israel mine inheritance." Isaiah 19:25.

Blessed be Africa, God's people and let the rod of curses be swallowed by the Rod of His true blessing. His Truth will swallow the Lie that has plagued her children and condemned them to endless ridicule. Let the blessing of the Lord turn the wheels of Africa's fortunes and princely Josephs be raised in her countries: those who fear the Lord and will enrich her people.

Africa's love for the Bridegroom has not escaped His observant eyes. In the Song of Solomon Chapter 1:5 she calls among His waiting virgins, "I am black, but comely, O ye daughters of Jerusalem, as the tents of Kedar, as the curtains of Solomon. Look not upon me, because I am black, because the sun hath looked upon me: my mother's children were angry with me, they made me the keeper of the vineyards, but mine own vineyard have I not kept. Tell me, O thou whom my soul loveth….."

And the Bridegroom calls back to her, "If thou know not, O thou fairest among women, go thy way forth by the footsteps of the flocks, and feed thy kids beside the shepherds' tents. I have compared thee, O my love, to a company of horses in Pharaoh's chariots."

The fiery hooves of war horses from Africa are coming! Every day as the voices of millions gather in Africa to worship and praise their Bridegroom, the sound of a massive company is heard. As Jeremiah 12:5 challenged those who sat at ease, "If thou hast run with the footmen, and they have wearied thee, then how canst thou contend with horses?" so does the challenge go out as they come. God is sending out from Africa a fiery company of heavenly horses that shall contend with the horses of the evil principalities of the lands. Their fearsome rumble sends terror into the enemy's camp and they run when no one is pursuing like the Syrians besieging Samaria did (2Kings 7:6). They fled in terror at the imagination of a hired cavalry of Egyptian and Hittite chariots! And wherever in the world her children are found gathered, they are known by the powerful energetic power of their praise. With the legendary terrible breeding of a company of horses in Pharaoh's chariots! Solomon found himself penning a song about a militant company of Kingdom warriors that he could only compare to war horses of the famous chariots of the king of the land of Ham!

As said before, the image of the suffering Saviour is represented by Ham. Outside Israel, Ham's children have suffered more than all their brothers in the story of man. They have even shared in the image of carrying Christ's cross up to Golgotha. When the devil sees black people he is constantly reminded of the sufferings of Christ, a constant reminder that out of that suffering came his defeat. The rise of the spiritual fervency of Africa's children adds to this fear. No wonder why his wrath is directed at her. So, whenever the bride from the land of Ham weeps, she should find comfort that she has been this honoured to share the sacrificial image of the Bridegroom.

Chapter 14
The third Man on the road to Emmaus (Luke 24:13-35)

Africa should be on the lookout for a mighty visitation of the Lord. Christ does not forget to reveal Himself to those He loves. When He chooses to reveal Himself to the suffering bride who has over the years been identified with His suffering and dying, He will only come when He is invited. The bride woos the bridegroom when she talks constantly about Him. The day is gone and evening is here. It is not the time to get discouraged.

Two men were walking to Emmaus. They had witnessed the power of the enemy destroy their hope and dreams of a Messiah who would scatter their enemies. They had waited for the day when a faithful redeemer would suffer at the hands of enemies but come out victorious to give back glory to their nation. After inconclusive reports of His resurrection, they must have lost hope in the scriptures. They were disappointed and discouraged like Africa.

The story of Africa and black people fits into the visionary psalm of David, Psalms 68. This psalm is an eternal prayer of those who wait for the Lord to show Himself as their deliverer from their many and strong enemies. Like Israel which is forever beset by enemies on every side, the prayer needs of Africa are just as eternal. Africa needs to repeat David's prayer, "Let God arise, let his enemies be scattered." (vs1.)

Sometimes Africa's despair is like that of Job who cried, "My days are past, my purposes are broken off, even the thoughts of my heart." Job 17:11. Whoever listens to the story of Africa on the news, hears debaters talking and listens to those who have lost hope, will see an Africa lying among the dead who God remembers no more. But those who will listen to the third man on the road to Africa will understand the secret of the man who died and rose again just as the scriptures say from Genesis to Revelations. He is the one who resurrected with the hopes and purposes of Africa. He is the one who will scatter her enemies.

Like a dead lion, Africa has remained the target of vultures. The mighty have fallen and the weapons of war perished from the once terrible of the nations of the world, a people terrible from their beginnings (Isaiah 18). The relentless plunder of Egypt's archaeology, graves and pyramids is almost symbolic of vultures feeding on the carcass of the once mighty kingdoms of Egypt/Ethiopia. The legendary kingdoms are now like the dead who lie in the ground with the princes of their land, judged by a great plague many years ago. And for years their hope in God had remained dead and waiting for the feet of the Prince of resurrection. Until He came and lived as a child among them. Until He died and arose again and breathed life into the dead. This was the promise that He would scatter their enemies. Africa can today declare, "Lo this is our God we have waited for Him, and He will save us."(Isaiah 25:9).

While Christ lay in the grave, the hope of man was lost. Those three days were the longest days in the history of mankind. He lay down there with the dead who have no hope. Because Christ had descended to the land of hopelessness that Job described as "the land of darkness and the shadow of death: a land of darkness, as darkness itself: and of the shadow of death, without any order, and where the light is as darkness." Job

10:21-22. The Psalmist in 88:5 calls it "Free among the dead, like the slain that lie in the grave, whom thou rememberest no more, and they are cut off from thy hand." For three uncertain days He lay there as testimony that Satan had prevailed over the plan of God. They would be born without hope, live a meaningless life and die without hope like beasts!

The two men on the way to Emmaus (Luke 24:13-29) were the image of despair from their disappointed hearts. They talked about the sad story of a good man who was killed by the Jewish leaders but of whom some reports suggested that He might have risen from the dead. Before the risen Christ revealed Himself to them, He was another story of hope deferred again that Africa is very familiar with. This image of a Jesus who may or may not have risen is what unbelieving teachers have given Africa. Like Israel, multitudes in Africa are still waiting for a messiah to rise and scatter their enemies. When their eyes open to see Him He is still the humble suffering saviour, faithful to save and the giver of glory. And unless they invite Him into their home, they shall welcome a new captivity by the false messiah who is soon coming to this world.

When Christ rose from the dead He demonstrated that He had disarmed the devil and his principalities and according to God's promise to Eve, her Seed had crushed the head of the serpent. The plans of the serpent for the kingdoms of this world were crushed. The plan of the serpent about every human being was crushed. The handwriting of ordinances that were written against us and in the devil's hand was blotted out by His blood (Colossians 2:14). When He returned to the Father He sat at God's right hand waiting till all His enemies would be put under His feet. Then He will be crowned King of all.

The good news to Africa is that the serpent's lies and accusations over her children have been crushed by Christ. The most stubborn of principalities that straddle the roads, the hills, the forests and the waters of Africa have had their heads crushed.

And the keys to the kingdom have been given to princes that Christ is raising all over the land. Africa should shout and rejoice everyday when princes of the Kingdom disarm principalities and powers by mass evangelism in the land. Africa should rejoice that princes endued with mighty power are bringing fire to the tongues of her people and giving them a pure language of faith, confidence and assertiveness in the word of God. The towers of prayers that rise everyday from the land of Cush are evidence that the enemy is in for a hard time from Africa. Some principalities are migrating from the heat of contest in Africa and moving to more comfortable environments in foreign lands.

Prophets like Isaiah and Zephaniah who saw the spiritual resurrection of Africa (Zephaniah 3:10) must have been astounded by the multitudes that raised their hands to God from all the lands beyond the rivers of Ethiopia. The picture was similar to the psalmist's description of the tribes of Benjamin, Judah, Zebulun and Naphtali with their people. The beauty of the tribes of Israel behind the singers and musicians praising God in Jerusalem can be translated to the princes from Africa who are bringing new tribes into the Kingdom of Christ to the praise of God in His city.

Let God arise, His enemies be scattered in Africa! Let the princes of the Kingdom declare the year of deliverance of Africa. Let them send emissaries to foreign lands who will shake the powers of ancient peoples who have forsaken the Lord. Let the uncompromising power of the kingdom bring the devil-apologetic preachers to their knees to declare that Jesus Christ is Lord. Wherever Ham's children carry the cross with demonstration of power, the mouth of sceptics and religious correctness shall be silenced.

The relentless spirit of the children of Ham has always unsettled the devil. This is the reason why the devil hates Africans. They have inside knowledge of the devil's evil machinery. They know his secrets. They have no doubt about his presence in this world. They do not apologise about upsetting his kingdom. After serving him with their fathers for many generations the children of Ham have now found the true power that is in Christ. With a vengeance they are going after every semblance of his power and in the name of their Lord scattering it all. The potential for damage that the children of Ham have over the devil's power is very significant indeed. They are pursuing the devil and his demons across continents with a violent and militant gospel, raising waves of revelation in this spiritual dimension.

Years ago in Harare, I listened to a young girl singing the hymn 'Abide with me'. She was a beautiful confident black girl. She reminded me of Solomon's black bride who her mother's children hated. But she sang beautifully and he loved her a lot. In the United Kingdom in 2009 I watched on TV how, before the football game at Wembley, a black choir sang the same hymn with the sweet and powerful voice of Africa. I was reminded of the three men who walked to Emmaus. The two said to the third Man 'Abide with us: for it is toward evening, and the day is far spent.' And the third Man went in to tarry with them.

There is also a road that leads to Africa. Two perplexed men are walking and talking about a Saviour. About One who alone can answer their questions. And Who alone can heal their despairing hearts. When the darkness deepens and helpers fade into the sunset, they call Him to arise and shine in their land. They call Him to abide with them forever, open their eyes and save them from their wretched and sinful state. From every village of Ethiopia, river, sea and island they raise their voices in song to thank Him for His amazing grace.

"Through many dangers toils and snares
I have already come
It was grace has brought me safe thus far
And grace will lead me home."

In September 2009 I was one of the multitudes on the road to Wembley to lift up our hands to the Man who had died and rose again. When the saints began to pray for the Lord to have His way, the glory of the Lord came down. The sound of praise was like the roaring of the waves of a mighty river. The virgin from the land of Japheth was there. The virgin from the land of Shem was there. And the 'black but comely' virgin from the land of Ham was there with her mother's daughters. One of her outstanding princes was there on an appointment from the Lord to bless her mother's daughters. The mantle of double anointing flowed like a river. And the Bridegroom was there to heal, comfort and love His Bride through His black virgin's hands.

END.

FAQs

Why should we believe the bible literally?

Not to do so is spiritual suicide. A black person, free from his traditional beliefs, but doubting the bible story is in danger of falling into the bible of evolution. You need more faith to believe that Darwin vocabulary than you need to believe the creation story. Anyone who believes the evolution bible will need to explain simple basic facts like how feathers evolved or how speech evolved. A hypothetical case of another Tarzan on an island of animals will produce a Tarzan who cannot speak no matter how old he grows. Just as Tarzan had to learn speech from someone, so has man. God gave man speech, not millions of years ago but only less than 10000 years ago. If man has been around for millions of years, where are their graves? We should be digging graves everywhere. By the law of averages, simple factorisation will prove that today's population of 6billion goes down to single digit parents about 7000 years ago. The world's resources themselves are so limited, everyone agrees. How could they have supported life for millions of years? Serious questions are being raised about carbon-dating in determining the age of things today. Evolutionists have been given free licence by a God-hating world to deceive man almost at will.

Why should we believe the author of Genesis?

Moses wrote Genesis. He was one of the most educated people in Egypt. It is sad when your next door neighbour or workmate thinks they are cleverer than Moses. Moses was a brilliant individual, much unlike how man-made movies want to portray him. The most important reason why we can believe Moses is that he was the only man in the bible known to have spent more time with God than anyone else. There were times he was in the presence of God for a 40day stretch. He is said to have had a personal knowledge of God no man before or after him ever had. Moses must have got the whole story of man from God himself and he had access to ask questions and get answers some of us would never get. God was writing the bible and He chose men for the hour and the purpose. People like Moses and Noah were much more intelligent than many people today who think they are smart. Some of the whiz kids of the world are found in the bible. It's time we threw out the image of sorry-looking old men with a confused and uncertain look that the movies have given us over the years. Individuals like Abraham were royal-like warrior patriarchs who were acutely aware of God's presence in their lives! And they were trusted to keep a proper record of the history of the nations to their children after them. We are deceived by our inventions today to presume that we are the cleverest of human beings. The precision to detail that the first books written by Moses presents is clear evidence of one of the world's most reliable authors. And it is also important to remember that God wrote the first ever words to begin the bible. The bible only begins after the tablets of stone given to Moses by God. After that he was assigned to write. By flashback storytelling technique Moses describes the account of the creation of the world and the distribution of all nations in just 11 Chapters, Genesis 1-11.

What skin colour then were bible people?

It does not appear like skin colour was an issue enough for the bible people to warrant it much of their writing ink. It is quite clear that Nimrod who was the founder of most of the cities in the present Iraq area was a Cushite and dark-skinned. How dark, no one knows. By the fact that he built six other cities beside Babel as far afield as Assyria, it does not look like Nimrod moved towards Africa after the dispersion. I am sure that the reason why Africa became known as land of the black people was because of the density of that colour in that area. It can be assumed that some dark-skinned people remained in the Mesopotamia areas or even beyond. The fact that today, countries like Iraq have a black population of about 2million may be evidence of East African slave trade over many generations and also remnants of dark-skinned groups who remained there after the dispersion.

Adam as a name means red earth and could indicate that Adam was of reddish colour. This would be ideal as less white skin has significant genetic potential for skin colour variations . The semitic term of used for Shemitic groups of people is based on their original mixed race look. Intermarriage has over the years made some Shemites almost white while some like those in Africa have retained significant mixed colour tones or even black colour with some needing DNA proof that they have Shemite roots. However the Shemites who look like Japhetic groups are always reminded by some racist Japhetic groups that they are not pure whites but Semitic.

The Egyptians were so proud of their black skin that the name Egypt is from this soil colour. They called themselves khemet and classified themselves by how dark one was. The darker one was, rightly or wrongly, the healthier they were considered to be. In some African groups today lighter-skinned fellow Africans are segregated against. The bible describes the Africans with titles like the "terrible from their beginning"

(Isaiah 18) and African mercenaries were valued and feared all over. The Greek writers wrote glowing accounts of the courage of black warriors as well. This pride could have contributed to the downfall of African power as foreign nations used their own strength against each other. Some writers suggest that Japhetic groups of nations could not have been able to colonise Africa without first stripping them of their strong men and women through slavery. As stated before, God knew best to have His bible written and sealed before man could bring race into it. No sense could have been made of the bible with today's racial overtones.

Skin colour and race did not feature significantly among early man. If anything, the darker-skinned Egyptians are on record as being prejudiced against the shepherd lifestyles of the Hebrews. Religion and lifestyle seem to have, to some extent, determined separation of groups of people unlike today when politics and scant resources dominate segregation. On the other hand the Jews were more prejudiced towards individuals who did not have their religious roots. The nations who founded societies were more educated about skin colour than our present day society. God's plan was of a colour-blind world where all the different human groups could live together, exercise their God-given dominion over the earth and exercise justice in fear of Him.

God had a complete picture of these nations in their ultimate habitation. He had also blessed them with the appropriate physical features suitable to live there. It is quite obvious that significant groups of the darker-skinned Cushite groups were driven by God's shepherd angels towards the hotter lands of Africa while the Japhetic lighter-skinned groups were driven toward colder climates. It is the devil's plan to discredit some nations by their skin colour and bodily features. Any nation who misses to see God's blessing in their physical looks will lose their confidence and curse themselves. The day you stop cursing your looks and begin to thank God, will be the beginning of your freedom from a self-made prison.

What colour was Jesus?

As we have noted, God ensured that the bible was written and completed before colour-conscious people could bring racial issues into prominence. The fact that baby Jesus and his parents lived among Egyptians of darker skin without attracting attraction could imply that if He was not very different from them. Egypt remains a country with a population of many shades of skin colour. His parents were Jewish and Semitic and it would be unusual if He was very different from them. A cursory reference to the skin colour of Jewish people is that of Moses in Exodus 4:6-7. When God demonstrated His power he turned Moses' skin "white" with leprous. If Moses was white, this would not have been peculiar. But when he was commanded by God to put his hand back in his bosom it is written that his skin colour was restored. I believe that like Adam whose name pointed to reddish clay colour, Jesus was not much different from him as the last Adam.By having Jesus born to Semitic parents, God may have ensured that the Saviour of all colours of people would neither be predominantly black or white. Above all, colour was not the important factor in Christ's mission to earth. Whether He was dark or light-skinned on earth is not important. His images, drawn by artists at their own time to appeal to their national pride, should not be used as the true image of Christ that no one really knows. He now abides in heaven in a glorified body which knows no colour. When we meet Him again, shed this outer skin and are translated like Him, then our heavenly bodies, like His own, will defy the trivialities of earthly skin colour.

Doesn't evolution help us to understand the bible?

We don't need evolution to understand the bible or to explain some parts of it. The reason why science has become valued by Christians is because it is now, more than ever, providing evidence of the existence of a very intelligent Creator. The continuous discovery of galaxies astounds scientists with the order in the universe. The big bang theory has been discredited even by children who know that if they hear a bang in their streets, they know that something caused it. Because even children know that Something or Someone must have started the bang. Scientists are also proving through DNA that we are all so intricately built .Only Someone more intelligent than we know was involved. Christians who believe evolution have a problem also believing some basic biblical truths like Noah's ark, crossing of the Red Sea, the story of Jonah, the virgin birth and even the reality of hell. They fail to grasp that God is not like them, that He is a far superior being to them.

Needless billions of cash are being wasted by man to try and disprove the existence of God through needless space travels. Many hungry people of the world would be fed from this waste if man only believed the simple bible account of God and creation. Only someone as callous as Satan would mislead man to waste so much resource meant for human beings to pursue another tower of Babel to try and reach God. If the resources of the world were fairly utilised, there would be no poor person on earth.

What is the role of archaeology in the bible story?

There are two groups of archaeologists: those who go out to disprove creation and those who want to find evidence to prove the bible story. Unfortunately the world's media ignores the discoveries of the second group and keenly promotes the first

God-denying group. The God-denying group look for the smallest evidence that suggests evolution and supremacy of some nations. Egypt's archaeology has been monopolised by racially persuasive archaeologists called Egypitologists . However, and more recently, scientists are showing a more balanced picture of how black people played a significant role in the bible story.

Where then did God come from?

When we are born into a world where things have a beginning and an end we can fail to grasp that there are some things that don't have to come in this pattern. God created us with a mind that is limited to this world and can effectively function within those limitations. Those things He has not made possible for us to grasp with our minds He has left it to His Word to reveal to us. There are some things about God we will never know until we leave this world. There are some things we will never see because our vision is limited by God to a specific dimension. If He had given us a different dimension we could easily see them but he knows that we don't need to see them in order to excel in this world. God lives in eternity where things do not begin or end. We are created beings who were put on a planet with a Time concept and timeframe and with all the resources we need.

Is it true that the fruit that Eve ate was having sex with the serpent?

The bible does not say that. There is no reason why Eve needed to have sex with the serpent before getting Adam involved because by now she had already had sex with Adam. They did not need the devil to teach them sex. God taught them sex because He is the one who ordained it in His creation. Sex is a great part of the love story of God and His creation. Without it man and woman would not comprehend the ecstasy of spiritual union with their Creator that they shall enjoy in eternity. If anything else, Adam should have observed animals having sex and should have seen from them. If sex was taught man by the devil, then sex is sin to this day. The most obvious thing is that Adam was a very intelligent man, strong and virile. His instincts took over as soon as he saw this wonderful body of a woman and his instincts overpowered him. We can easily believe that the two of them were in each other's arms as soon as God left them alone just as normal adults drawn by love and desire for each other do. God made them love each other and desire each other. The reason why the bible refers to Adam 'knowing his wife' and bearing Cain was by the style of the writer who prioritised issues as he wrote them. There is also a hint that God was responsible for the first family planning that took place. He left childbirth till the test of the forbidden fruit. Otherwise Adam would have had children who differed in nature. Those before the fall would not have his fallen nature while those after his fall would have his fallen nature. Adam called Cain the first born of humanity.

If God is alive, why is there so much violence?

As long as the devil is in this world violence will increase. The devil has deceived many people into believing that he does not exist. The devil has no problem with a world that believes in the existence of God. He has a problem with a world that believes in the existence of an evil devil. As long as the world believes in a non-existent devil or a comical image of one, he can create as much havoc as he wants on earth. The devil is the opposite of God, trying to copy God and to misrepresent God. One sign of the end of the world will be increased violence levels like in the days of Noah. Revelations describes unimaginable levels of bloodshed that shall befall this world. Those who are angry with God for bloodshed levels today should read their bibles again. When God allows the nations to use their weapons which they have perfected and prided themselves with over many years, then the fallout shall be incomprehensible.

God is both the God of love and of judgement to extreme levels. If we find it hard to question our earthly bosses, who do we think we are to question such a fearsome God?

Why do the evil people prosper more than the good people?

The world is founded on its own laws that glorify evil as good. Justice can never be expected to be universal in this kind of world. From the days of Cain who killed his brother Abel but received a mark to protect him from justice, evil murderous and cunning people have their place in this world. Those who suffer abuse and murders are also assured a place in this world. That is the world's inheritance from Adam's first children. Only the coming kingdom of Christ shall change that.(See Cain project)

Why should we pray?

Praying sounds silly to the unsaved. Science has given us increased awareness of the unseen world. The fact that we can make a phone call on mobile and communicate with someone thousands of miles away without using visible telephone lines proves the wonder of scientific invention. There is another wonder called prayer. It does not use satellite systems. It uses spiritual satellite. As soon as we switch on our spirit to pray, the network of the Holy Spirit triggers the more advanced lines of heaven. Prayer becomes a form of recharging ourselves or emergency fusion with higher source of power needed to change natural laws or enemy power. Prayer therefore is the right we have to get God to intervene in natural laws or laws that the enemy is enforcing. God's answer to prayer comes as a favour or significant change in prevailing circumstances. Therefore praying is a right we can exercise or not. Our enemy will never leave us alone and we will find that because of this we will need to learn God's words and ways to get His intervention for each crisis. We also find that we often ask God to get involved in issues to do with our loved ones. As we grow more confident in prayer we find ourselves praying for other people and events. In this way we become intercessors. If we ask, the Holy Spirit empowers us more and gives us His language or tongue to pray on our behalf or on behalf of others.

How do I find God?

Access to the world of internet requires passwords. Unless you get the password right, you do not get access into the computer. By similar analogy, God has restricted access to His kingdom to only one word; Jesus. That is the only Password He accepts. Those who use other passwords and get access to some kingdom are not in the Kingdom of heaven. There are many kingdoms that the devil and man have created that use a variety of passwords. Do not be deceived. Jesus is the only Password to God's kingdom.

Solomon the renowned poet and songwriter answered one of his most beloved black brides, "If thou knowest not, oh fairest among women, go thy way forth by the footsteps of the flock, and feed thy kids beside the shepherd's tents." 1:8. There are footsteps that lead in the direction of those who have followed Jesus the true Shepherd. These are the footsteps of those people that have heard His voice. They will lead you to a good flock. There are many shepherds' tents that Christ is raising in every city and village. If you stop long enough you will hear the word of God. Jesus will cover you with His love and be your Lord. Pray this short prayer."Jesus I want to know you. For many years I have followed the knowledge and wisdom of this world but my life is not satisfied. You are the Tree of life. Please cover my nakedness with your blood and clean me of my shameful deeds. I receive you into my life Lord Jesus. Make me a child of God today." You will be amazed of the change that will miraculously begin to take place in your life. It is called the miracle of being born again.

NOTES (optional reading)

PART TWO

Chapter 1
God is love: His story is a story of love

The central theme of the bible story is love. Love of an Eternal Lover and His creation called Adam. According to the bible the name Adam was a name that spoke of the oneness of Adam and Eve. They had one name. To God a man is a living soul in a male body while a woman is a similar living soul in a female body for the purpose of reproduction and of sharing the experience of the ecstasy of union of spirits that only heaven can offer. Adam is the one who named his wife Eve. And he was the one who decreed that the two would be one flesh. God used human love to develop this concept of love. He shared His bridegroom role with Adam and Eve was the first bride of the heavenly love affair played on the earthly stage. The concept of this eternal relationship was based on two fundamental principles: respect and love. As long as the creature respected God, His authority and laws, His love would be assured to cover them and bless them.

Adam and Eve were naked but covered by God's love. Love is the most powerful cover in existence. Because of this love they were protected from hatred and curses. Hatred was non-existent in this world of love and they were naked/innocent to it. The emotion of hatred was not known where perfect love was.

When the devil used the serpent to get Adam and his bride to disrespect God, he introduced them to a new awareness. The cover of God's covenant love and blessing was no longer assured as before. They suddenly grew aware of a new shortcoming in their lives. God made the enormity of this loss of His cover of love over them felt by them in a new awareness of nakedness they had not known. This awareness would remain a sign they would never forget. Nakedness remains a constant reminder to humans of profound failure. Today it is only allowed as a sign of love and worship between a married man and woman.

Adam obeyed his wife but disobeyed God. Adam, the first bridegroom loved his wife so much that he was disobedient unto death for her. Cain was their first child. They gave birth to hatred itself and curses. Adam must have been the first priest to his family to reach out for God's love through sacrifices and blood of animals. This method of reaching out to God would continue until Christ the obedient last Adam would restore God's covenant with man and out of His body would be created a new Bride called the church made up of virgins from all nations. Christ loves this Bride and was obedient to God unto death for her. It is still up to the church to be wise and respect her Husband so that she does not go about naked like the Laodecian church (Revelations 3:15).

The eternal love story has been played throughout the bible. God has allowed other individuals to act out His love for His creation as we shall see. Abraham and Isaac were lovers whose brides told an eternal story. Sarah is given as an example of the respectful wife who called her husband 'lord'. She is the eternal image of Jerusalem, the mother of all the wise virgins of Christ. Rebekah's faith and courage to leave her home with a stranger for a foreign home and marry her bridegroom Isaac, is symbolised with the Bride of Christ lifted to the heavens to meet her Bridegroom, Jesus Christ.

Unlike Adam, Abraham and Isaac were not prepared to love their wives unto death and each denied their wives when faced with death-threatening situations. Maybe they had fresh memory of Adam who lost everything for the love of his wife and were afraid to risk God's call for their wives. But God confirmed their wives' own calling by intervening with great signs.

The story of Jacob's two brides was also used to play the salvation story. Jacob is central to the story of both Jews and Gentiles. He and his brother Esau share some basic quality as twins. Jacob shared his brother's trait to be duped and by way of this trait the blessing of Messianic blessing was passed on to Gentiles. The veil of darkness that hid Leah's face on Jacob's wedding night has ensured that Gentiles get their rightful week of wedding bliss with the groom before the chosen Israel gets her turn.

Jacob used the weak/dark vision of his father Isaac to get Esau's blessing. The sin of deceit and its dues was spared him because his mother Rebekah, who initiated the deceit asked to bear the blow for him.(Genesis 27:13) What happens to Jacob after this incident should not be lightly treated as just rewards for his deceitful nature because his mother rightfully paid her son's debt. She did not live long to meet her beloved Jacob again.

Jacob is the familiar face of many of us; cunning, taking advantage, yet quite gullible when we meet our betters. After fleeing into exile with nothing in his hands, he gets enriched by God's blessing on his life and his father's blessing. He falls head over heels in love with Rachel and she, like Esau, expected to get her rightful blessings. She expected to be Jacob's elder wife. But using Jacob's deceived vision and cover of night, Laban transferred that blessing to Rachel's elder sister Leah. What Isaac's chosen elder son Esau had lost, Laban's elder daughter got. She even got the burial at Jacob's side in the sepulchre of patriarchs and their wives at Machpelah while Rachel was buried near Bethlehem. That must have evened the ground in God's court of justice.

It is the story of these two brides of Jacob that sums up God's plan for the Jews and Gentiles. Out of her that was not beloved, Leah, would be born Judah, from whom the line of the Messiah would come. The children of the outsiders (Gentiles) would receive Him as the Bridegroom. By the time the veil of night would be gone, Rachel the chosen mother of Israel would only be allowed to the Bridegroom's chambers after the Gentiles have fulfilled their 'full week' of celebration with the Bridegroom.

Paul makes it clear in Romans 11 that when the time of the Gentiles is finished, God will turn to Israel. Through Leah flowed God's grace to the Gentiles while Israel's mother Rachel, like her idolatrous descendants hundreds years later who died in the wilderness before reaching the land of the Messiah, also died before reaching Bethlehem, the city where the Messiah would be born. (Jacob had decreed that whoever had Laban's idols should die, unaware that his beloved pregnant Rachel was sitting on them.) Out of Rachel flowed the foundation of Israel as a nation through Joseph. But her role as the chosen wife of Jacob also encompasses the Gentiles. Her first son Joseph is given to bless the Gentiles represented by Egypt. Out of her second son Benjamin, comes Paul the apostle to the Gentiles.

The brides of Solomon who was the Temple builder, wisest and richest king of Israel are the fitting actresses of the age-old love song. He was driven to dwell on his love with the bride from the descendants of Ham who describes herself as black but comely and who he describes as outstandingly beautiful. Like Christ, he had brides from all parts of the world but unlike Christ he was a king and not a shepherd. He failed to shepherd his people in the ways of God. His wives did not respect him or his God and led him astray. Christ is Shepherd first and King next. He feeds his Bride in His word and leads her in the paths of righteousness. The black bride in his song is seeking more the shepherd part of her lover than the militant one. Israel missed the Shepherd Bridegroom because she was looking for the kingly/militant bridegroom. But the black bride ends up with both the shepherd and king in her Bridegroom.

Through the prophets God refers to Israel as His unfaithful wife. In often touching style He despairs of her disrespect for His laws and her disregard for loving her through a special covenant not given to other descendants of Adam. Whenever Israel did right, God praised her with loving words and blessings.

A telling account of His love was when He used the prophet Hosea to play His role of the loving and forgiving Husband. In the bible book of Hosea, Hosea lives the experience of marrying a prostitute bride, flood her with showers of presents and words of affection. Even after she flees from him he plays God's love to buy her back from her lovers, clean her and garnish her. God used Hosea's human feelings and emotions to role-play His love for His Bride.

It is not surprising that the first miracle Jesus performed was at a wedding in Cana. His ministry was a marriage in itself. Those who question whether Jesus ever married miss the point of His ministry. Christ had a Bride to betroth. For more than three years He prepared the ground to establish His Bride the church. He gave several parables about marriage and wedding to underline this.

In Ephesians 5 Paul expertly explains the mystery of marriage as representing the Eternal bridegroom and His wife the church. He repeats the balance of love and respect as the heavenly standard of Christ's spiritual union with His wife. In every act of intercourse where love is lacking, no real fulfilment is found while lack of respect makes loving difficult. Because many marriages lack the fragrance of love as expressed in the model love Song of Solomon, we often miss the intensity of the love of Christ for His Bride. We also fail to represent the true relationship of Christ and His Church.

John concludes the revelation of the marriage of Christ and His church in their eternal union of New Jerusalem while the bridegroom (antichrist) of the wicked bride called Babylon destroys his own bride in Revelations 17. The Bride is received into the glorious world of the eternal love of Her Bridegroom, to a world where love is the breath and song of existence and where there is no curse of hatred anymore. The story concludes with these words, "And the Spirit and the bride say, Come." (Revelations 22:17.) This concludes the bible story of the Eternal lover and His redeemed Bride.

Chapter 2
The Cain project

As we observed above, Cain was the first symbol of the curse of hatred with a human face. The devil has managed to overcome the world with powerful, big brother-like nations who kill, lie about it and oppress their brothers. These nations have lost the fear of God and the conscience of their fathers. The children of Ham have been endlessly abused by these Cain nations and Cain leadership wherever they turn. Even those who have found the grace of salvation still need to rise up and assert themselves against these powers.

Jesus said something very powerful to the Pharisees that gives us insight into the complex problem that the devil has imparted to man. He said to them, "You are of your father the devil, he was a murderer from the beginning and a liar…" John 8:44.These big brother custodians of the Law were just as dangerous to the birth of the kingdom of heaven as the spirit of Cain is to all dedicated children of God. The devil had it all planned from the beginning.

After getting Adam and Eve thrown out of Eden, the devil was waiting for a foothold in their family. He laid his claim on Cain, the strong-willed elder brother of every human being, who was the pride of his parents, the testimony of God sharing His creative and spirit-sharing power with man. His name incidentally means a spear, a weapon of war, maybe signifying his father's hope that Cain would be the spear of the family, to defend it and protect it. The bible makes it clear that Cain was the very firstborn of Adam and Eve. It was God's own infinite knowledge that had kept Adam and Eve from conception of a child until they had been tested. (They would not be the only ones to be tested. God's story with man in the bible is built on similar tests of obedience.) The story of man would have been complicated with children from their fallen state and those from their innocent state. (The suggestion that the forbidden fruit was a sexual act between the serpent and Eve is as petty as it is ridiculous. Adam was cleverer than most of us and definitely did not need the serpent to teach him the God-ordained act of procreation! The bible writer knew the difference between a fruit and a sexual act.)

The Cain traits in Adam's children

Cain had no fear of God in him. The way he answered God showed that. Jude describes the hard words of a generation of people who he compares to Cain. That generation is here, of people who make comedy with God's name. The antichrist generation shall be money-greed stout-faced people who do not give a toss about sacred things.

Cain was driven by anger and hatred. It is difficult to comprehend how an individual can be driven by hatred in their day to day interaction with you. Individuals who have a loving or friendly character can fail to understand how a generation of people can be driven by hatred of someone's colour, someone's looks, someone's origin and someone's achievements. The combination of anger and hatred has been responsible for a lot of bloodshed in this world.

Cain's biggest problem was his pride. Though God warned him about the danger of his vengeful spirit, Cain ignored correction and proceeded to kill Abel. He did not repent after

God confronted him but instead was more concerned about the enormity of judgement given to him. After getting reprieve for the murder, he did not repent to his parents or to God. In a record that dwelt more on male children than females, Cain married one of his sisters,(Genesis 5:4) left his family and went east, away from the face of God. Cain was so self-assured of himself that he chose to separate himself from his family and their God. He is an example of this generation that does not care about mother or father or their God: a generation that minds their own business and hopes you mind your own. The bible calls this a vagabond lifestyle.

The world has been alarmed by the Cain-type of elder brother masquerading as leaders of society. They love bloodshed, and don't care about being their brother's and sister's keeper. They worship the god of weapons like the name of their namesake Cain/spear. They do not acknowledge God in their leadership and instead have sold their hearts to the devil to whom they sacrifice the fruits of their cursed labour. The ground is cursed for their sakes and under their leadership many become poor.

Cain had had the option to either follow his brother's exemplary sacrifice or seek his father's advice to rectify the situation. The freedom of choice remains for every human being to this day. He chose the advice of the evil one.

Like his parents before him, Cain chose to obey Satan instead. However he went a step further to allow Satan control over him and killed his brother. Then like the devil, he lied to God that he did not know what had happened to his brother. Satan stood by waiting, knowing that God would judge Cain for this. Satan knew God's character, that He judged rebellion without fail. He himself had been thrown out of heaven by the same God for rebellion.(Isaiah 14:12-17).Satan knew that he had won claim of Adam's first- born son, at the same time killing his second son. He must have watched with pleasure as he heard

God cursing Cain. The curse would give him the right to control Cain's descendants and assign his demons to their lives. Cain became the first son of the devil.

After this, Adam and Eve gave birth to another son who they named Seth. Eve said that this son was God's replacement for Abel (Genesis 4:25). In due time, a God-fearing generation stretching to Noah's family was born from Seth. So by the time of the Flood two significant lines of Adam's descendants lived on earth: one with a righteous thread in it through Seth and the other with an evil thread through Cain.

Satan began to establish his character in Cain's children. One of his grandchildren Lamek became the first bigamist recorded in the bible. Women's names feature prominently in his line of descendants, being the mothers of very gifted individuals who invented musical instruments and the use of metals (Genesis 4). Whether these gifted children were a result of the recorded sexual relations between "sons of God"(Genesis 6) and beautiful daughters of man, is not clear. (However the bible says that Satan was an excellent musician himself (Ezekiel 28:13). The bible says that this forbidden sexual union produced legendary gigantic offspring.

Cain's descendants who were all destroyed in the flood must have had significant influence on Seth's descendants too, considering how evil overtook the world over a period of about 1500 years, that only eight individuals from Seth's generation survived the Flood. Normal human behaviour will suggest that a lot of knowledge and skills from Cain's generation were also passed on to the generation after the flood. And the behaviour of those people must also have been passed onto surviving generations. One of them is the curse that Cain inherited for humanity as the first born of humanity. It was marked by God's mark on his forehead. Some preachers teach that Cain's curse is similar to that of Ham. We have already noted that this is not true.

Chapter 3
The original curse that hangs over nations

Africa's curses, like the curses of all nations of the world, are founded on an age-old base. Zechariah 5 makes it clear what curse the world should worry about. It is the curse of the flying roll.

Written on both sides, the terrifying roll hangs over the whole earth between heaven and earth, as a testimony to both heaven and earth. On one side, Zechariah says, is written the curse for the thief and on the other the curse for those who swear falsely. Swearing falsely includes false religions and false churches. This curse resembles a woman in an ephah/tub- like container who is sealed inside the ephah by a heavy lead seal. The woman is called Wickedness and two powerful women with stork-like wings fly her to a destination in Shinar/ Babel/Babylon in present day Iraq. She is made the cornerstone of her new home in that land. This home is a semblance of the curse that the devil brought to this world. This vision of Zechariah appears to reveal how the foundation of Babylon was laid long ago. (It is sad that the original home of man has become the devil's base of his resemblance of man's wickedness.)

The use of measured equipment in the vision may signify a judgement that is measured and sealed for the appropriate season. The storks may signify the appointed time. Jeremiah 8:7 says of the stork, "The stork in the heaven knoweth her appointed times, and the turtle and the crane and the swallow observe the time of their coming, but my people know not the judgement of the Lord."

The people of this world also do not know their judgement. They are clever at judging other nations and believe that God will not judge their own wickedness. But their wickedness is sealed and the name Babylon is the semblance of the city on which this Wickedness is built. Wickedness is the name by which God calls this woman in Zechariah 5. In Revelation 16 her secret is revealed and her judgement follows in Revelations 17 and 18.

However, Zechariah 5:3 makes it very clear that the judgement of this woman is based on two sides of the flying roll. He says, "This is the curse that goeth forth over the face of the whole earth: for every one that stealeth shall be cut off as on this side according to it: and every one that sweareth shall be cut off as on that side according to it."

The eternal wickedness of the earth is summed up as the wickedness of theft and that of lying/swearing falsely. The wealth of Babylon in Revelation 18 is described as built on this wickedness. The wealth of the wicked is stored in Babylon. The monetary system of this world, its banks, stock exchanges etc is designed on a Baylonian model. The first murder was written on the theft of Abel's life and Cain swearing falsely about his brother's whereabouts.

Beginning with Africa, it is quite obvious that serious levels of theft are practised every day. Many curses follow common theft in the villages and cities. Corporate theft has cursed the continent with corruption. Laws have been made in communities and government to make evil look right and justify stealing. Exiles in foreign lands bite the hand of their hosts by engaging in fraud and stealing money by devious means while justifying their actions as a way of recovering what has been stolen from Africa. By doing this they are transferring curses to African communities where they use the money to build homes, support relatives and engage in other activities. Men and women steal each other's bodies and swear that they have done no sexual evil. Churches use tricks to steal money from people and swear by bible scripture that they are doing it for God. When the church should be working to remove the curse of the world, it is sometimes found adding to the curse by working in Babylon. God warns his people to flee from Babylon (Revelations 18:4).

Africa has suffered from the scourge of foreign theft. They have stolen Africa's children into slavery and stolen her resources. They have put in place laws and international institutions to justify their wickedness and no one can win against them. Some have used the word of God to justify this theft. They have amassed massive wealth built on the two pages of the roll. According to Zechariah 5 this curse has descended onto the very foundations of their homes. Their kingdoms shall crumble like those before them who stole and swore falsely.

It is not Africa only that has suffered from this scourge but she is the most common image of this scourge at its worst. Many nations of the world have suffered as well. Africa has been like an open book everyone has had the freedom to read while other nations have stayed on the shelf sealed and unread. But bit by bit the books of other nations are opening and sadly they are not very different at heart from Africa. The institutions of theft have been planted strategically all over the world. Controlled by individuals of acute wicked intelligence in some regions of the world, they siphon away the resources of the poor and subject nations to unceasing labour and despair reducing them to the level of benefits recipients. It is not only Africa that has poor and deprived people. All societies of the world have their own fair share of the destitute whose dignity has been eroded by the spirit of greed. The only difference between a dictator impoverishing his people and the CEO of a multinational organisation who impoverishes nations is their titles. Corruption is in the blood of human beings irrespective of their colour. The only difference is that while Africa's corruption is recklessly obvious to see, that of some powerful nations is usually clandestinely concealed. Recent political and economic shocks have revealed corruption and greed in developed countries that were never before imagined. God can humble any nation that thinks itself purer than others.

Theft is driven by greed and covetousness. And greed is given a human face when laws and books are used to justify it. The most powerful demon in the world is the demon of greed. It comes across as a business executive with a suit and tie. Behind it follows the demon of warfare and strife. The devil has used greed to entice our ancestors. Let us retrace this process of enticement briefly.

God instructed Adam in the garden to eat every other tree except the tree of good and evil. Eve must have spent long hours looking at the forbidden fruit wondering what it tasted like. Adam too must have pondered the same issue judging by what little persuasion he needed to eat the fruit when Eve eventually succumbed to the deceit of the devil. Satan deceived man through his propensity for greed. He was clever enough to notice that vulnerable point of man.

The last Adam, Jesus, overcame greed by beginning His ministry with 40 days of fasting. That's God's ordained method of overcoming the spirit of greed. The first curse came through greed.

Satan used the same weapon of greed against Noah. Noah drank a little more than he should, a bit more, until he lost his senses. People still find it hard to respect hopelessly drunken individuals. A lot of people end up apologising profusely after drunken episodes. Satan, first and foremost, embarrassed Noah and demeaned him to himself. The story of the life of this great man of God would always be littered with this embarrassing episode. This episode nearly cost him his son Ham to the devil.

Esau was another individual who lost his birthright to Jacob because of greed for a pot of stew. Like the other legendary overconfident hunter Nimrod before him, Esau's right to lead the nations to the gate of heaven was taken from him and given to Jacob. At Luz/Bethel Jacob saw the spiritual staircase to heaven in a dream. There God revealed Himself to him and gave him a revelation of a blessing that would reach all nations of the world. Jacob exclaimed, "How dreadful is this place! This is none other but the house of God, and this is the gate of heaven."(Genesis 28:17) Esau had lost the honour to bring together the nations to a place where heaven descended to touch the world and not where the earth ascended to touch heaven like in Nimrod's Babel.

It is easy to trace the role of greed and how it was used by Satan to get a foothold in the affairs of man. Most obvious examples are the curse of the quails in the wilderness journey of the Jewish group of the sons of Shem when for the greed of meat they invoked wrath over their nation. Psalms 78:30-31says, "But while their meat was yet in their mouths, The wrath of God came upon them and slew...them."

In a horrible twist to this saga of greed Jesus used greed in reverse to expose the devil in Judas. Here He was, the Tree of life in person, offering His body and blood to the world again. Satan too sat there behind Judas to partake of the first ever experience of this kind since the Garden of Eden. Jesus reversed the curse of that greed by offering Judas the morsel. Suddenly the devil sitting between them was exposed by his own greed and disappeared into the darkness to fulfil his role. The last

Adam had literally given the devil the taste of defeat that he had delivered to man in Eden.

The curse that hangs over man is also a part of our fallen self. It is the fallen Adam and Eve trying to live again in the kingdom of heaven when we accept Christ. God showed less sympathy for Ananias and Saphira who tried to enact the Adam and Eve deception in His newly redeemed Eden/church of His Son. They failed to muzzle their greed and stole what they had pledged and in the process swore falsely. The Holy Spirit used Peter to send an eternal message that He would judge everyone who brought the works of Babylon into His church. They died instantly (Acts 5). God would not tolerate another Adam and Eve rebellion in the new Vineyard of His Son, the last Adam. The bible warns his church to stay out of Babylon and her lifestyles (Revelations 18).

Babylon's king/husband is Lucifer and to them shall be born a child who shall put a mark on people's foreheads. And by a God-allowed delusion, the nations that have all along rejected the true Messiah, and moved away from the face of God, will embrace this thieving and swearing messiah. Then the age-old battle between blessings and curses will be concluded: the mystery of the two ladies who rule the hearts of the sons of man.

Chapter 4
Lady of the nations (Babylon) vs New Jerusalem

Babylon and Jerusalem stand out in the bible as the mothers of two distinctly opposite generations of people. The Cain-like generations who promote lifestyles of sin and curses have given their souls to Babylon while the Abel-like God-fearing and God-worshipping generations have given their souls to Jerusalem. While the eternal home of the Abel generation is a New Jerusalem in heaven, the eternal home of the Cain generation is the lake of fire. The three sons of Noah have had equal parts to play in the story of these two cities.

Ham's son Cush birthed Nimrod who founded physical/political Babylon. He passed it on to Shem's children characterised by a mixture of Chaldean, Arab groups and many similar descendants who transformed Babylon into a spiritual base of all Jesus-denying faiths according to their given role of promoting spirituality. Closely bound with Japheth who Shem shares his tent with, the task of enlarging Babylon's influence over the world has been pedalled by Japhethic nations. Japheth and Shem's power and wealth-management skills have significantly enlarged Babylon into an economic lady of the nations signified by trading cities built on all the strategic ports of the world.

On the other hand, the Jebusites, descendants of Canaan, Ham's son, founded physical Jerusalem. Shem's descendants, the Hebrews, turned Jerusalem into the spiritual and salvation base of the world to which the Saviour was sent to die for the world. Jerusalem has remained the battleground of powerful world faiths spurred by Shem's descendants. Japheth's role in Jerusalem has both enlarged Jerusalem's spiritual power over the world and at the same time enlarged her into a city that determines the economic and political destiny of nations of the world.

Created on the sixth day, man was given two choices. God had breathed into him an integral eternal and undying part of Him called His spirit. That is part of Him related to the Tree of life in the garden whose eternal home is New Jerusalem (Revelation 22:2.) The soulish and fleshly part of his lust is signified by the tree of Babylon's lusts (Revelations 18: 14). By choosing the lust of his fleshly pleasures, man inherited the curse of his labour in a cursed ground. The law of God to Moses limits the days of man's labour to six days. Man's sacrifice of this labour from the cursed ground was rejected by God in Cain's hands. The devil has since laid claim to the labour of man who had chosen him. The fruit of man's labour is stored in a city built on a shaky base of Wickedness that the bible calls Babylon. Man's false religions, which are an unacceptable sacrifice to God are like the strange stork-winged women that lift her up.

Babylon is given the image of a woman. This could have its origin in the female image of human creation, Eve, who the devil deceived first and who lusted after the forbidden fruit. Having observed how much power the woman image had over Adam, the devil grew obsessed with her. John himself in Revelations 17:6 says that when he saw the woman Babylon he wondered about her with great admiration. Any human being who denies sometimes admiring the world of Babylon and her children is not being honest. The pleasures of this world are so overwhelming that without constantly fighting them, we could lose our salvation. The devil knew that with the image of the woman he could destroy God's plan. The record of prominent women in Cain's genealogy is pointing to the role he attached to the female image.(This should not be confused with the God-ordained role of woman in society). Other angelic beings related to him, called the sons of God, increased the obsession by marrying the female image of creation and bearing evil giants with them. A vanity woman's image would be a reminder of this spirit in the earth. This image fills vanity media images of the lost world today. It is the image of females whose only occupation is being vain enough to be powerful.

However, God also used the image of woman to destroy the devil's plan. By specifically pointing to the woman as the source of the Seed that would crush Satan's head, He promised redemption of the image of the woman. Then by creating the last Adam, Jesus, through the woman figure of Mary without involving a man's sperm cell/seed, He ensured that the woman had effectively given Adam the Seed that would return to him the covenant she had caused him to lose in Eden. That's why another image of a woman resembling righteousness is seen flying in Revelations 12. She is given wings to fly like an eagle and is the mother of a Child of righteousness, Christ, who shall rule the nations. God effectively redeems the role and image of the woman in the story of the children of Adam.

Man's labour over all generations and his increased knowledge of good and evil and religion will not attain the righteousness of God. Even the great wealth of God's mirror nation of Israel when the epic symbol of human labour was recorded as 666 pure gold talents during Solomon's famous glorious kingdom (2 Chronicles 9:13) was the most exploitative of regimes. After Solomon's death the people rebelled when his chosen successor, Rehoboam, ignored their pleas for labour reduction (1Kings 12:1-19). And even Israel at its best was a symbol of wicked fleshly pleasures as symbolised by Solomon's many women. And though he had built and dedicated God's first temple, and wrote some of the best wisdom ever, he despaired of all his experiences and knowledge of good and evil and called it vanity of vanities. Indeed man's labour and wisdom without Christ is vanity of vanities.

The summary of man's labour, pleasures and religiosity in Babylon is a weariness that is vanity of vanities. It falls short of God's purity through Jesus Christ the new spiritual temple builder who built it in only three days of His death and resurrection. The most that Israel, at the height of her glory and with the laws of the true God could show, was to defile God's temple and defile themselves with many women like their king.

The image of the curse/wickedness is said to hang over the whole earth though her resemblance is based in Shinnar (Iraq). Therefore the image of the Chaldean Babylon in Shinnar was a testimony of the presence of a living curse that is symbolised by a productive woman, capable of birthing children. In her grows the tree of the knowledge of good and evil. She has given birth to many other cities of wickedness throughout the world. Many of today's cities are founded on the pleasure-loving sinful lifestyles of Babylon. Babylon has given birth to cities that are economic capitals controlling greed, religious capitals of Christ-denying cities, Christian capitals of heresy and wealth-driven churches, among others. The Babylonian merchants are also still obsessed with Nimrod's dream of building the highest skyscraper to touch the gate of heaven.

Babylon has been able to give her children a false sense of rebirths at different levels of civilisation. The Renaissance, for example, was a rebirth of arts which ushered in a new wave of wisdom and knowledge that gave nations a strong and enduring sense of rebirth. As far as they were concerned nations felt reborn and have missed the true rebirth through Christ. Every rebirth has given nations reason to be absorbed in self-glory. The Industrial revolution was a rebirth of invention and standards of living that ushered in a new status quo of developed and underdeveloped nations giving rebirth to pride of nation and race. This revolution has given many nations reason to be absorbed in themselves without needing Christ. This has seen the birth of Babylon's child called racism which has bewitched many proud people and absorbed them in serious delusion.

National independence of many developing nations, including Africa, has seen a rebirth of national identity and self-determination that brought with it nations more absorbed in their nationality than with a rebirth in Christ. Babylon will continue to give her children knowledge, ideas, traditions and feelings that will keep them absorbed with themselves more than with seeking Christ. A most recent rebirth is the resurgence of Babylon's arts of witchcraft that is targeted at young people through books, games, cartoons and children movies.

Babylon's children believe in a world speaking with one tongue as United Nations to be the answer to the future of the nations of this world. Her king/husband is called Lucifer, another name for Satan (Isaiah 14). Giant merchants, musicians, so-called stars, and various children of this world are being born out of this union: whose lifestyles are based on the lusts and pleasures of Babylon. They will be forerunners of the last kingdom of the antichrist.

On the other end a resemblance of the redeemed woman would be built on mount Zion in Canaan, a land that belonged to the cursed son of Ham. This was God's testimony that He would renew His cursed creation by His own blessed blood. The image of Jerusalem would be testimony of the righteousness of God all over the world built on the image of blessings that is heavenly New Jerusalem. Her image is that of the blessed woman of Revelations 12 who is given wings to fly from her enemies. In her grows the Tree of life. Her king/husband is God Himself and she births children all over the world. These valiant, Spirit-filled children of the kingdom will run with the message of the Lord and prepare for the kingdom reign of Christ.

The judgement of the woman or the lady of the God-forsaking world will only be revealed at the end of man's kingdoms. The number of completeness, 7, is given for the heads of the kingdoms over which she has ruled in the history of man (Revelations 17:3). The mystery of the unity of the wickedness of the nations and this woman is at last revealed. The antichrist/beast of Revelations 13, endued with the power/crowns of the most powerful 10 nations of the time will be the product of their long affair.

In a sudden twist to her fortunes the judgement will befall her. The curse that has clung to her walls and beams will eat her. Her cursed children, 10 nations will eat her flesh. Just as the wicked Cain gave a despicable sacrifice of the product of the cursed earth, this Cain-like beast will preside over the sacrifice of Babylon's satellite cities. The labour of men and the ill-begotten wealth of the sinners shall crush and their lifestyles too. Revelations 18 describes their lamentations. The time is short and the devil's team has no time with frivolous human pleasures. Typical with his nature, Satan has no use for men's pleasures: he has always wanted God's throne in Jerusalem. He knows what Truth is but will destroy all semblance of worship, declaring himself only worthy of worship.

Those who rejected Christ as their Messiah will welcome this new messiah, inviting judgement like that which befell Egypt. They will be deceived to welcome a messiah who will not give his life for his disciples but will betray all their deluded expectations. Then the eyes of many shall be opened to see who the devil really is and how deceived they have been over many generations. Through a period of unprecedented cruelty, generally accepted as tribulation, that the devil will unleash on humanity through his antichrist, the nations that decide to turn to Christ will do so through bloodshed. Israel appears to be the missionary of this wave of repentance to Christ (Revelations 14) with the fire of revival engulfing the children of Ishmael and Esau among other Shemite groups. The fervency of these groups will bring about massive revival in the world and complete God's redemption plan for mankind. God will again crush the devil's plans and age-long deception over nations. The devil's violence and cruelty will make the elect in the nations to turn to the Messiah they had denied and a stampede on the Kingdom with the violent virtually taking it by force.

As Cain cunningly invited his righteous brother Abel out to the fields, the beast will lure repentant Israel and the world with smooth words of deceit. To the killing fields of Jehoshophat (Armageddon) he will lure the nations to destroy the righteous. Revelations 19 shows Christ intervening at the nick of time as He returns to earth to judge the beast and his armies. The devil is cast into a bottomless pit and the antichrist and his false prophet/disciple are cast into the lake of fire. The kingdom of Christ is then revealed that will span years of a just society of God's glory on earth.

The children of Shem will be there. The children of Ham will sing and dance forever. And the children of Japheth will open their arms to welcome their brothers as their equals in the kingdom. For the Lord shall rebuke the nations and rule them with a rod of iron (Revelation 12:5). He will teach them the ways of God and give them the kingdom that was prepared for them from the beginning.

The bible sums up the fall of the mighty human kingdoms and how their greed will be judged by God. It also offers words of comfort to the exploited of this world that there is a new world order coming to the world. The kingdoms of this world will become the kingdoms of our God and the wealth of these kingdoms will be transferred over to Christ and his saints. (Revelations 11:15 and Daniel 7:27). It is called the time of the reign of Christ: the kingdom when all questions will find answers and curses will be found no more.

Revelations 19 describes the marriage of the Lamb and His wife. That is the consummation of the song of love that His wise virgins from the whole world have sung with Him over all generations. And the black virgin who sings with the beauty of the legendary Shulamite and with the stately beauty of the horses of Pharaoh's chariots will be there. And her heavenly Solomon will not be led astray by his wives, but He shall lead them through a glorious kingdom where they shall rule with Him and after that, through all eternity. An eternity where there shall be no curse (Revelations 22:3) but where the blessings and glory of the Lord shall reside.

Hebrews 12: 22-24 sums up the journey of those sons and daughters of Adam who are redeemed through a new covenant without a curse in it. It says, "But you are come unto mount Sion, and unto the city of the living God, the heavenly Jerusalem, and to an innumerable company of angels, To the general assembly and church of the firstborn, which are written in heaven, and to God the Judge of all, and to the spirits of just men made perfect, And to Jesus the mediator of the new covenant, and to the blood of sprinkling, that speaketh better things than that of Abel."

Chapter 5
From the Middle East to Africa

The material used in this Chapter is quite speculative. I have used ideas from reflection, discussion and reasonable assumptions to trace the footsteps of black people in Africa from the Flood plains of the Middle East. From creation to Babel, the area occupied by man was what was historically known as the Mesopotamia. The bible says that the Babel project was started when the united descendants of Noah led by Nimrod were travelling from the east, suggesting that their ancestors had been deposited there by the ark after the Flood. They seem to have been populating the land as they moved back west towards the land of their origin around the Euphrates/Tigris area. The dispersion was a miraculous occasion as God drove them apart to all directions of the earth He wanted populated.

Nimrod the Cushite is said to have founded five more cities around this area including Nineveh of the Assyrians. It must be understood that these cities have archaeological records that show brilliant architecture. These people were not Stone Age men. There could have been other families who chose to live a primitive existence in the neighbourhood whose records have come up with some archieological discoveries.(We still live side by side with groups of people who for one reason or another choose to live a primitive life. Present day forest tribes in Africa, Brazil and Papua New Guinea are an example. Archaeological discovery of such a community in an area does not necessarily reflect that the whole community was primitive at that time.) God-denying archaeologists have tended to use such disparities to generalise historical dating, while at the same time abusing their licence to carbon dating.

The bible shows that God ordained leadership in all nations who had skills in nation building. Founder fathers of nations have never ceased to amaze later generations with their advanced knowledge. This pattern seems to repeat itself in our generation. The people who have made impact on civilisation are not the many but the few. The rest tend to sit in the glow of these gifted individuals or their ethnicity. The prevalence of education and information sharing has made it possible for the rest to share quickly in the knowledge of the gifted few and increase the pace of development. Without advanced means of sharing knowledge and information, many nations have tended to digress to very low levels of existence as in some African groups.

The easier group to trace from Mesopotamia were Ham's grandchildren by Canaan. Their land was named after them in the present day areas of Israel, Lebanon, Jordan, Gaza etc. Ham's grandchildren by Mizraim can easily be traced to Egypt where they founded the present day land of Egypt. Ham's son Phut settled in the area around Libya and was founder of the people in that part of North Africa. The footsteps of Ham's son Cush, from whom most of black Africa descends, are a bit difficult to trace. That's why I have employed reasonable assumptions in my views.

The fact that Nimrod founded six cities in the Mesopotamia area could have led his group of dark-skinned people to originally dominate in that area. The fact that the colour-denoting name of Cush was used after this son of Ham meant that other groups may have been lighter in skin than him. But that did not mean that he did not intermarry with these other groups. The assortment of different shades of colour in that part of the world may explain this. Nimrod must have been the king from a dark-skinned people who dominated politics in that part of the world. But that did not preclude other groups from challenging his authority as time went by. History shows evidence that leaders were removed by new leaders and new clans. It is probable that over the years, Nimrod's dynasty was removed by other groups and feeling threatened in this way moved away from the Mesopotamia area. The Sumerian dynasty that followed seems to have been a mixture of Shem's descendants who by the term semitic looked mixed race in colour.

The Syrians were a Shemitic group from whom the Hebrew group of Abraham originated. Abraham was probably Syrian by descent. The Chaldeans who ruled Ur from which Abraham was called could have been a mix of Shem's descendants and Cush. Many Shemites appear to have travelled further east to places like India, Pakistan, Afghanistan. The present day Iran and Iraq remains a mix of the descendants of the three children of Noah with Japhethic /Caucasian groups well represented.

The bible gives indication that Japhet's Caucasian descendants moved towards the islands of Elisha, Javan and as far afield as Tarshish (Spain).The families of Gog, Magog, Meshech, Torgamah spread east and north to populate Europe, Soviet Union, China, Korean peninsulas and Japan. The very hot climate of man's original home must have been too much for Japheth's lighter-skinned descendants while Shem's and Ham's less-lighter and darker-skinned descendants found it more bearable. Noah had also blessed Japheth to be enlarged (Genesis 9:27) and he had more sons than his brothers suggesting how diverse his descendants and population sizes would be. Fair/light-skinned Japhethic descendants might have been the first to move to colder climates compatible with their skin while a mixture of brown and Semitic nations whose skin could tolerate the hot weather have remained in the Middle East.

Intermarriage continued to shape the new nations though it is quite obvious that God in His own wisdom and as He had planned, brought about predominant genes in the greater population of that nation. It is quite obvious that God had in His plan people shaped as Oriental, Caucasian, Negroid or of mixed features. Genetic impurities in many colours of people may also support the fact that God dispersed groups from Babel according to differences in tongues only, not in colour differences. He had prepared for each of them places that they would find compatible with their body features. They did not need to evolve at all to get to that stage. However, the continuous changes in skin colours and densities through intermarriage remains evidence that this process was responsible for the looks of original founder groups.

There are some authors who push for the view that all original founder people were black. That may sound politically persuasive to black people but most black people are not uncomfortable to accept that other people did not have to look like them. A God who created people different is quite comfortable with black people as long as other non-black people accept that. The problem arises when non-black people try to colour God after themselves and relegate others to lesser creations. The idea of an Adam who was red earth is scientifically correct. Brownish/ reddish clay is the colour of usual clay or clay in the Mesopotamia area from which God created Adam. That is the kind of skin that could scientifically produce the genetic variations that have populated the earth.

In tracing the footsteps of the Negroid group of people who populated Africa it is reasonable to remind ourselves that Cush was dark-skinned in order to be called Cush. While the name Ham also means brown, whether all of Ham's children were dark is debatable. But Cush is the father of the dark-skinned people of Africa. Africa is home to different dark skin shades. Within one family, a very light-skinned brother can be born next to a very dark sister or vice-versa. Should lighter-skinned individuals marry, their children may grow significantly different from those of the darker-skinned who marry within the darker skin group. Very light Negroid groups of Africans like the San and the Khoi-San of South Africa are an example. Some darker groups of Africa are known to be strongly inclined towards preserving the darker shade of their descendants to the extent of discouraging intermarriage with lighter skin shades.

Whether the Cush groups left the Mesopotamia area after the dynasty of Nimrod ended or before, is not known. The growing population in the area must have caused friction and competition for resources which led to a form of mfecane/crushing of tribal groups. The Cush groups found their way to the coast of Africa either by trekking or by ship or boats. Ship-building must have been an art known by descendants of Noah who had built the biggest floating vessel hundreds of years before. This could in part explain how different shades of skins found themselves on islands in the Pacifics for example. Settlement was mainly on river basins like the Niger, the Blue Nile, the Zambezi etc. Rivers were so important that the bible so often described nations by their rivers. Eden itself was described by its rivers. Interior lands in Africa are described as 'beyond the rivers of Ethiopia'.

Africa is described by two main names in the bible: Egypt and Ethiopia. A passing look at the map of Africa and the Middle East will show why these two names featured mainly in describing Africa. They are the most obvious entry points by which Africans must have reached Africa on their way from Mesopotamia. They could have steadily migrated through Canaan's land via Egypt before moving southwards or westwards. Or they could have come by way of Saudi Arabia through Yemen and sailed the narrow waters of the Red Sea at that point onto present day Ethiopia before spreading out to the immediate north, westwards or southwards.

Bantu groups in Zimbabwe claim their ancestry to East Africa from where they dispersed. One interesting original name of their homeland in Africa is Tanganyika, now known as Tanzania. In Shona dialect Tanganyika literally is Tanga(begin) nyika (land) which could imply it was their original home when they reached Africa. The legend of the Great Zimbabwe ruins suggests biblical structures inherited from Babel. Incidentally Tanzania is close as entry point to Ethiopia and also accessible by boat from the East.

It sounds like Egypt and Ethiopia were the first destination/entry points of Cush's into Africa. Due to their ease of access these two have also grown into targets for occupation by a mixture of nations. A pattern of relatively lighter- skinned African groups at the coastlines of Africa is evident of intermarriage with other lighter-skinned trader foreign groups of nations whose descendants went on to become the dominant groups. Some of them today deny they have African blood in them. As the socio-political pendulum swings towards the dominance of lighter-skinned individuals in many nations of the world, the original skin colour of the founder people of nations has grown distorted.

As suggested above, settlement was around rivers from where the growing populations spread out to all parts of Africa. The strongest kingdoms seem to have been centred around Egypt as we know it today and Ethiopia (Greek name for land of people of (sun) burnt faces). The latter is supposed to have included present day Sudan (Arabic name for dark-skinned) which was famous as the Meroe kingdom south of the Nile. Ethiopia may not have been the size of Ethiopia we know today but could have been known to describe the land dominated by dark-skinned people. There are suggestions that Saudi Arabia itself including Yemen/Sheba was land populated by dark-skinned people during bible times and could have been part of greater Ethiopia.

Stronger groups of Africans appear to have settled to develop formidable armies and stable cities and traded extensively with other communities, whereas the weaker moved to the interior areas where they built poor dwelling structures they could easily discard of if they were forced to move on by stronger groups.

Significantly weaker groups who came together due to one genetic deficiency of growth eg pygmies and bushmen/San almost descended to a semi-primitive existence as they moved constantly from stronger groups. The San/Bushman of Botswana left typical rock paintings as they migrated south from sub-Saharan Africa. For the pygmies, the dense forests of Africa became a welcome protective environment.

The African hut was as symbolic as the tent of the Shemites who were just as nomadic. Both represent insecurity in this world, a living testimony that this world is not our home. Instability in Africa has encouraged this kind of nomadic dwelling. The colonial policies of arbitrary movement of black people from their ancestral areas also reinforced this feeling of insecurity. There has been significant change in the nature of the kind of homes that more settled groups of people in Africa, sure of their political and economic security are building nowadays. However in less secure nations shacks have replaced huts as evidence of this insecurity.

Africa south of the Sahara was like the Garden of Eden, well nourished with good rains, good soils, green vegetation, fruit and all kind of animal life. The hunting skills that the Africans had learnt from Nimrod now came into full play. A lot of precious energy and time got wasted in hunting at the expense of development. For centuries Africans were, by abundance of resources, some of the most blessed people in the world.

The generosity of Africans which has been famed as bordering on recklessness has rendered them open to exploitation by more hungry and thrifty foreigners. The ready availability of resources in the land made the African groups less dependent on one another for survival. This encouraged defragmentation of strong and united communities leading to weak sub-clans which were easily divided by slave traders. Africans became early victims of slavery in this manner. The children of Shem trafficked them from the east while centuries later Japheth's children ravaged them from the west. This must have been discussed to some extent in various Chapters of this book.

This Chapter has been used to interpret the history of black Africa's migration from the land of the origin of man. As stated in my introduction, reasonable assumptions have been used in reaching these deductions. These are to some extent backed by historical facts and broadly suggested by the word of God.

END.

BIOGRAPHY

Artiel was born on 8 January 1956 in rural Chivi to a school headteacher and his wife a shop owner. He grew up in a well-to-do family and could have passed as a spoiled kid at schools and college. His country of birth, Rhodesia, was a colony until 1980 when it became known as Zimbabwe after independence. Artiel trained as a schoolteacher due to the limited choices of careers during colonial days and taught for 12 years. At the same time he was more dedicated to the things of God in his local church of Zimbabwe Assemblies of God where he had found Christ at 20 years of age, leaving behind a life of traditional demonic worship and membership to a missionary church that did not teach new birth or the power of the Holy Ghost. He is grateful for the leadership of Dr Ezekiel Guti who is the founder of Zaoga and has remained a great influence in his life. He developed a strong prayer life, leading prayer groups and praise teams over many years. He remains a loud voice calling for dedicated intercessors to this day. He has been married to his wife Tsitsi for 29 years.

Artiel is a gifted individual who wrote a very touching novel about a disabled boy 'Grandmother's child' for which he won 1st Prize at Zimbabwe International Bookfair 1995. He also wrote three booklets entitled 'Arise, Shine' on the call to more prayer, 'Comfort ye comfort ye my people' on dealing with stressful situations, 'Shades of Memories' a poetry for Christian lovers.

He also produced a praise CD with the help of his eldest son Dean entitled 'Power Choruses.' His talent in drama and film is shared by his youngest son Michael who is studying film and media at present while his daughter Rabecca has taken after her mother's social qualities and studying Social Work. Artiel is presently based in United Kingdom where he has trained as a health practitioner and stands as a pillar devoted to serious intercession.

Artiel's experiences in colonial Zimbabwe and his shared identity with the history of African people have given him the passion he displays in this book. He draws a lot of his reference from living with deprived people in Africa and from the experiences of black people in the diaspora.

Artiel has been a church elder for many years and supports several ministries in rural Zimbabwe and Nigeria.

SD - #0035 - 060826 - C0 - 216/138/11 - PB - 9781844268115 - Gloss Lamination